PRAISE FOR
WEB SECURITY FOR DEVELOPERS

"Reads easily and provides essential knowledge to aspiring web developers."
—HELP NET SECURITY

"The biggest advantage of this book is that it collects all a developer needs to
know in one space . . . This solid work should be relevant for years to come."
—SCOTT J PEARSON

"A good resource for developers at any level to fill in the holes in their knowledge or reinforce their existing expertise."
—JON LAZAR

WEB SECURITY FOR DEVELOPERS

Real Threats, Practical Defense

by Malcolm McDonald

no starch press

San Francisco

Printed in the United States of America

Third printing

26 25 24 23 22   3 4 5 6 7

ISBN-10: 1-59327-994-9
ISBN-13: 978-1-5932-7994-3

Publisher: William Pollock
Executive Editor: Barbara Yien
Production Manager: Laurel Chun
Production Editors: Katrina Taylor and Meg Sneeringer
Cover Illustration: Gina Redman
Interior Design: Octopod Studios
Project Editor: Dapinder Dosanjh
Developmental Editor: Athabasca Witschi
Technical Reviewer: Cliff Janzen
Copyeditor: Sharon Wilkey
Compositor: Danielle Foster
Proofreader: James Fraleigh
Indexer: BIM Creatives, LLC

For information on distribution, bulk sales, corporate sales, or translations, please contact No Starch Press, Inc. directly at info@nostarch.com or:

No Starch Press, Inc.
245 8th Street, San Francisco, CA 94103
phone: 1.415.863.9900
www.nostarch.com

Library of Congress Cataloging-in-Publication Data

```
Names: McDonald, Malcolm, author.
Title: Web security for developers / Malcolm McDonald.
Description: San Francisco : No Starch Press, Inc., [2020] | Includes
index.
Identifiers: LCCN 2020006695 (print) | LCCN 2020006696 (ebook) | ISBN
9781593279943 (paperback) | ISBN 1593279949 (paperback) | ISBN
9781593279950 (ebook)
Subjects: LCSH: Hacking. | Computer networks--Security measures.
Classification: LCC TK5105.59 .M4833 2020 (print) | LCC TK5105.59 (ebook)
| DDC 005.8/7--dc23
LC record available at https://lccn.loc.gov/2020006695
LC ebook record available at https://lccn.loc.gov/2020006696
```

[S]

To my wife Monica, who put up with being
ignored on weekends while I wrote this book,
and my cat Haggis, who contributed content
by walking over my keyboard periodically

About the Author

Malcolm McDonald is the creator of *hacksplaining.com*, one of the most popular security training resources for web development on the internet. He has spent two decades writing code for financial firms and start-ups, and drew on his experience as a team lead to produce straightforward, easy-to-grasp tutorials about security vulnerabilities and how to protect against them. He lives in Oakland, CA with his wife and cat.

About the Technical Reviewer

Since the early days of Commodore PET and VIC-20, technology has been a constant companion (and sometimes an obsession!) to Cliff Janzen. Cliff is grateful to have had the opportunity to work with and learn from some of the best people in the industry, including Malcolm and the fine people at No Starch. Cliff spends a majority of the work day managing and mentoring a great team of security professionals, but strives to stay technically relevant by tackling everything from security policy reviews to penetration testing. He feels lucky to have a career that is also his favorite hobby and a wife who supports him.

BRIEF CONTENTS

CONTENTS IN DETAIL

4
HOW WEB SERVERS WORK   23

5
HOW PROGRAMMERS WORK   35

PART II: THE THREATS   47

6
INJECTION ATTACKS   49

ACKNOWLEDGMENTS

I would like to thank all the folks at No Starch Press who massaged my words into some sort of readable form: Katrina, Laurel, Barbara, Dapinder, Meg, Liz, Matthew, Annie, Jan, Tyler, and Bill. Thanks to my colleagues Dmitri, Adrian, Dan, JJ, Pallavi, Mariam, Rachel, Meredith, Zo, and Charlotte for constantly asking "is it done yet?" Thanks to Hilary for proofreading the first chapter! Thanks to Robert Abela at NetSparker for setting up the website sponsorship. I'm grateful to all those who pointed out typos on the website, you are the real heroes: Vinney, Jeremy, Cornel, Johannes, Devui, Connor, Ronans, Heath, Trung, Derek, Stuart, Tim, Jason, Scott, Daniel, Lanhowe, Bojan, Cody, Pravin, Gaurang, Adrik, Roman, Markus, Tommy, Daria, David, T, Alli, Cry0genic, Omar, Zeb, Sergey, Evans, and Marc. Thanks to my Mum and Dad for finally recognizing that, yes, I have a real job now that I have written a book, and I don't just "do stuff with computers." And thanks to my brothers Scott and Ali, who are sadly not published authors, despite all their fancy PhDs and such. Finally, one last thanks to my wife Monica, who has been extraordinarily patient and supportive throughout the writing of the book. And thanks to Haggis for mostly staying away from the keyboard and only occasionally puking on the couch.

INTRODUCTION

 The web is a wild place. It's easy to get the impression that the internet was designed very deliberately by experts and that everything works as it does for a good reason. In fact, the evolution of the internet has been rapid and haphazard, and the things we do on the network today go well beyond what the original inventors imagined.

As a result, securing your website can seem like a daunting proposition. Websites are a unique type of software that is available to millions of users immediately upon release, including an active and motivated community of hackers. Big companies routinely suffer security failures, and new data breaches are announced every week. How is a lone web developer supposed to protect themselves in the face of this?

About This Book

The big secret of web security is that the number of web vulnerabilities is actually rather small—coincidentally, about the size to fit in a single book—and these vulnerabilities don't change much from year to year. This book you will teach you *every* key threat you need to know about, and I will break down the practical steps you should take to defend your website.

Who Should Read This Book

If you are a web developer who is just starting out in their career, this book is an ideal hitchhiker's guide to security on the internet. Whether you have just finished a computer science qualification, are fresh out of bootcamp, or are self-taught, I recommend you read this book cover to cover. Everything in this book is essential knowledge, and it is explained in the most straightforward manner with clear examples. Preparing fully now for the threats you will face will save you a lot of trouble down the line.

If you are a more experienced programmer, this book will prove useful too. You can always benefit from brushing up on your security knowledge, so use this book to fill in any gaps you may have. Treat it like a reference book and dip into the chapters that seem interesting. You don't always know what you don't know! Seasoned programmers like yourself have a responsibility to lead their team by example, and for web developers, that means following security best practices.

You will notice that this book isn't specific to any particular programming language (though I make various security recommendations for the major languages as needed). A sound understanding of web security will benefit you, no matter which language you choose to program in. Many programmers will use a variety of languages across the course of their careers, so it's better to learn the principles of web security than to focus too much on individual libraries.

A Brief History of the Internet

Before I lay out the contents of the book, it will be useful to recap how the internet arrived at its current state. A lot of clever engineers contributed to the explosive growth of the internet, but as with most software projects, security considerations often took a back seat while features were added. Understanding how security vulnerabilities crept in will give you the context you'll need when learning how to fix them.

The World Wide Web was invented by Tim Berners-Lee while working at the European Organization for Nuclear Research (CERN). The research conducted at CERN consists of smashing subatomic particles together in the hope they will split into smaller subatomic particles, thus revealing the essential fabric of the universe, with the understanding that such research has the potential to create black holes right here on Earth.

Berners-Lee, apparently less interested than his peers in bringing about an end to the universe, spent his time at CERN inventing the internet as we know it today, as a means of sharing data between universities about their findings. He created the first web browser and the first web server, and invented HyperText Markup Language (HTML) and the HyperText Transfer Protocol (HTTP). The world's first website went online in 1993.

Early web pages were text-only. The first browser capable of displaying inline images was Mosaic, created at the National Center for Supercomputing Applications. The creators of Mosaic eventually went on to join Netscape Communications, where they helped to create Netscape Navigator, the first widely used web browser. In the early web, most pages were static, and traffic was transmitted without encryption. A simpler time!

Scripting in the Browser

Fast-forward to 1995, and a recent hire of Netscape Communications named Brendan Eich took 10 days to invent JavaScript, the first language capable of being embedded in web pages. During development, the language was called Mocha, then renamed LiveScript, then renamed again to JavaScript, before being eventually formalized as ECMAScript. Nobody liked the name ECMAScript, least of all Eich, who claimed it sounded like a skin disease; so everyone continued to call it JavaScript except in the most formal settings.

JavaScript's original incarnation combined the clumsy naming conventions of the (otherwise unrelated) Java programming language, the structured programming syntax of C, the obscure prototype-based inheritance of Self, and a nightmarish type-conversion logic of Eich's own devising. For better or worse, JavaScript became the de facto language of web browsers. Suddenly, web pages were interactive things, and a whole class of security vulnerabilities emerged. Hackers found ways to inject JavaScript code into pages by using cross-site scripting attacks, and the internet became a much more dangerous place.

A New Challenger Enters the Arena

The first real competitor to Netscape Navigator was Microsoft's Internet Explorer. Internet Explorer had a couple of competitive advantages—it was free and came preinstalled on Microsoft Windows. Explorer rapidly became the world's most popular browser, and the Explorer icon became "the internet button" for a generation of users learning how to navigate the web.

Microsoft's attempts to "own" the web led it to introduce proprietary technology like ActiveX into the browser. Unfortunately, this led to an uptick in *malware*—malicious software that infects users' machines. Windows was (and remains) the primary target for computer viruses, and the internet proved an effective delivery mechanism.

Internet Explorer's dominance wouldn't be challenged for many years, until the launch of Mozilla's Firefox, and then by Chrome, a snazzy new browser created by the plucky young search startup Google. These newer browsers accelerated the growth and innovation in internet standards. However, by now, hacking was becoming a profitable business, and any security flaws were being exploited as soon as they were discovered. Securing their browsers became a huge priority for vendors, and website owners had to keep on top of the latest security news if they wanted to protect their users.

Machines for Writing HTML

Web servers evolved at the same rapid clip as browser technology. In the first days of the internet, hosting websites was a niche hobby practiced by academics. Most universities ran the open source operating system Linux. In 1993, the Linux community implemented the *Common Gateway Interface (CGI)*, which allowed *webmasters* to easily create websites consisting of interlinked, static HTML pages.

More interestingly, CGI allowed HTML to be generated by scripting languages like Perl or PHP—so a site owner could dynamically create pages from content stored in a database. PHP originally stood for Personal Home Page, back when the dream was that everyone would run their own web server, rather than uploading all their personal information to a social media behemoth with a questionable data-privacy policy.

PHP popularized the notion of the *template* file: HTML with embedded processing tags, which could be fed through the PHP runtime engine. Dynamic PHP websites (like the earliest incarnations of Facebook) flourished across the internet. However, dynamic server code introduced a whole new category of security vulnerabilities. Hackers found novel ways to run their own malicious code on the server by using injection attacks, or to explore the server's filesystem by using directory traversal.

A Series of Tubes

The constant reinvention of web technology means that much of today's internet is powered by what we would consider "old" technology. Software tends to reach a point where it works enough to be useful, then falls into "maintenance" mode, where changes are made only if absolutely necessary. This is particularly true of web servers, which need to be online 24/7. Hackers scan the web for vulnerable sites running on older technology, since they frequently exhibit security holes. We are still fixing security issues first discovered a decade ago, which is why in this book I describe every major security flaw that can affect websites.

At the same time, the internet continues to grow faster than ever! The trend for internet-enabling everyday devices like cars, doorbells, refrigerators, light bulbs, and cat-litter trays has opened a new vector for attacks. The simpler the appliance connecting to the Internet of Things, the less likely it is to have auto-updating security features. This has introduced huge numbers of unsecured internet nodes that provide a rich hosting environment for *botnets*, malicious software agents that can be installed and controlled remotely by hackers. This gives an attacker a lot of potential firepower if they target your site.

What to Worry About First

A web developer can easily be discouraged by the difficulties involved with properly securing a website. You should have hope, though: an army of security researchers are out there bravely discovering, documenting, and fixing security flaws. The tools you need to secure your site are freely available and generally easy to use.

Learning about the most common security vulnerabilities, and knowing how to plug them, will protect your systems against 99 percent of attacks. There will always be ways for a very technical adversary to compromise your system, but unless you are running an Iranian nuclear reactor or a US political campaign, this thought shouldn't keep you up at night.

What's in This Book

The book is divided into two parts. Part I covers the nuts and bolts of how the internet works. Part II delves into specific vulnerabilities you need to protect against. The content is as follows:

Chapter 1: Let's Hack a Website
In this introductory chapter, you will learn how easy it is to hack a website. Hint: it's really easy, so you did well to buy this book.

Chapter 2: How the Internet Works
The "tubes" of the internet run on the Internet Protocol, a series of network technologies that allow computers across the world to communicate seamlessly. You will review TCP, IP addresses, domain names, and HTTP, and see how data can be passed securely on the network.

Chapter 3: How Browsers Work
Users interact with your website via the browser, and many security vulnerabilities manifest there. You will learn how a browser renders a web page, and how JavaScript code is executed in the browser security model.

Chapter 4: How Web Servers Work
Most of the code you will write for your website will run in a web server environment. Web servers are a primary target for hackers. This chapter describes how they serve static content, and how they use dynamic content like templates to incorporate data from databases and other systems. You will also dip into some of the major programming languages used for web programming, and review the security considerations of each.

Chapter 5: How Programmers Work
This chapter explains how you should go about the process of writing website code, and the good habits you can develop to reduce the risk of bugs and security vulnerabilities.

Chapter 6: Injection Attacks

We will begin our survey of website vulnerabilities by looking at one of the nastiest threats you will encounter: a hacker injecting code and executing it on your server. This often happens when your code interfaces with a SQL database or the operating system; or the attack might consist of remote code injected into the web server process itself. You will also see how file upload functions can allow a hacker to inject malicious scripts.

Chapter 7: Cross-Site Scripting Attacks

This chapter reviews attacks used to smuggle malicious JavaScript code into the browser environment, and how to protect against them. There are three distinct methods of cross-site scripting (stored, reflected, and DOM-based), and you will learn how to protect against each.

Chapter 8: Cross-Site Request Forgery Attacks

You will see how hackers use forgery attacks to trick your users into performing undesirable actions. This is a common nuisance on the internet, and you need to protect your users accordingly.

Chapter 9: Compromising Authentication

If users sign up to your website, it's essential that you treat their accounts securely. You will review various methods used by hackers to circumvent the login screen, from brute-force guessing of passwords to user enumeration. You will also review how to securely store user credentials in your database.

Chapter 10: Session Hijacking

You will see how your users can have their accounts hijacked *after* they have logged in. You will learn how to build your website and treat your cookies securely to mitigate this risk.

Chapter 11: Permissions

Learn how you can prevent malicious actors from using privilege escalation to access forbidden areas of your site. In particular, if you reference files in your URLs, hackers will try to use directory traversal to explore your filesystem.

Chapter 12: Information Leaks

You might well be advertising vulnerabilities in your website by leaking information. This chapter tells you how to stop that immediately.

Chapter 13: Encryption

This chapter shows how to properly use encryption and explains why it is important on the internet. Be prepared for some light mathematics.

Chapter 14: Third-Party Code

You will learn how to manage vulnerabilities in other people's code. Most of the code you run will be written by someone else, and you should know how to secure it!

Chapter 15: XML Attacks

Your web server probably parses XML, and could be vulnerable to the attacks described in this chapter. XML attacks have been a consistently popular attack vector among hackers for the past couple of decades, so beware!

Chapter 16: Don't Be an Accessory

You might unwittingly be acting as an accessory to hacking attempts on others, as you will see in this chapter. Be a good internet citizen by making sure you close these security loopholes.

Chapter 17: Denial-of-Service Attacks

In this chapter, I will show you how massive amounts of network traffic can take your website offline as part of a denial-of-service attack.

Chapter 18: Summing Up

The last chapter is a cheat sheet that reviews the key elements of security you learned throughout the book, and recaps the high-level principles you should apply when being security-minded. Learn it by heart and recite the lessons before you go to sleep each night.

1

LET'S HACK A WEBSITE

 This book will teach you the essential security knowledge you need to be an effective web developer. Before getting started on that, it's a useful exercise to see how you would go about attacking a website. Let's put ourselves in the shoes of our adversary to see what we are up against. This chapter will show you how hackers operate and how easy it is to get started hacking.

Software Exploits and the Dark Web

Hackers take advantage of security holes in software such as websites. In the hacking community, a piece of code that illustrates how to take advantage of a security flaw is called an *exploit*. Some hackers—the good guys, commonly called *white hat hackers*—try to discover security holes for fun, and will advise software vendors and website owners of the exploits *before* making them public. Such hackers often collect a financial reward for doing so.

Responsible software vendors try to produce patches for *zero-day exploits* (exploits that have been publicized for less than a day, or not publicized at all) as soon as possible. However, even when a software vendor releases a patch to fix a software vulnerability, many instances of the vulnerable software will remain unpatched for some time.

Less ethically minded hackers—*black hats*—hoard exploits to maximize the time windows during which they can use vulnerabilities, or will even sell the exploit code on black markets for bitcoin. On today's internet, exploits get rapidly weaponized and incorporated into command line tools widely used by the hacking community.

Solid financial incentives exist for black-hat hackers who use these exploitation tools. Black markets for stolen credit card details, hacked user accounts, and zero-day exploits exist on the *dark web*, websites available only via special network nodes that anonymize incoming IP addresses. Dark websites, like the one pictured in Figure 1-1, do a brisk business in stolen information and compromised servers.

Figure 1-1: Hi, yes, I would like to buy some stolen credit card numbers since you are clearly a high-level Russian hacker and not an FBI agent hanging around the dark web as part of a sting operation.

Hacking tools that can take advantage of the latest exploits are freely available and easy to set up. You don't even have to visit the dark web, because everything you need is a quick Google search away. Let's see how.

How to Hack a Website

It's remarkably easy to get started hacking. Here's how to do it:

1. Do a Google search for **kali linux download**. *Kali Linux* is a version of the Linux operating system specifically built for hackers. It comes preinstalled with more than 600 security and hacking tools. It's completely free and is maintained by a small team of professional security researchers at Offensive Security.

2. Install a virtual container on your computer. *Virtual containers* are host environments that allow you to install other operating systems on your computer, without overwriting your current operating system. Oracle's VirtualBox is free to use and can be installed on Windows, macOS, or Linux. This should allow you to run Kali Linux on your computer without too much configuration.

3. Install Kali Linux in the container. Download and double-click the installer to get started.

4. Start up Kali Linux and open the Metasploit framework. *Metasploit*, as shown in Figure 1-2, is the most popular command line tool for testing the security of websites and checking for vulnerabilities.

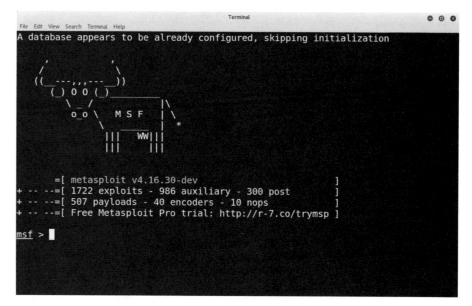

Figure 1-2: Hacking can be achieved only with sufficient ASCII-art cows.

5. Run the wmap utility from the Metasploit command line on a target website and see what vulnerabilities you can find. The output should look something like Figure 1-3. The wmap utility will scan a list of URLs to test whether the web server exhibits security flaws. Make sure you run the utility only on a website you own!

```
                                              Terminal                                        _  □  x
 File  Edit  View  Search  Terminal  Help
 + -- --=[ Free Metasploit Pro trial: http://r-7.co/trymsp ]

 msf > load wmap

 . - . - . - . - . - . . - - - - . - - - .
 |  |  |  |  ||  |  |  |  ||  |  ||  |-'
 `----'`-'-'.'.'`-^-'`-'
 [WMAP 1.5.1] ===   et [   ] metasploit.com 2012
 [*] Successfully loaded plugin: wmap
 msf > wmap_sites -a https://50.63.202.8
 [*] Site created.
 msf > wmap_targets -t https://50.63.202.8
 msf > set DOMAIN hacksplaining.com
 DOMAIN => hacksplaining.com
 msf > wmap_run -e /root/.wmap
 [*] Using profile /root/.wmap.
 [-] NO WMAP NODES DEFINED. Executing local modules
 [*] Testing target:
 [*]     Site: 50.63.202.8 (50.63.202.8)
 [*]     Port: 443 SSL: true
 ===========================================================
 [*] Testing started. 2018-03-25 05:17:34 -0400
 [*] Loading wmap modules...
```

Figure 1-3: Hacking engaged—expect a visit from law enforcement imminently.

6. Pick an exploit in the Metasploit database that will permit you to take
    advantage of the vulnerability.

    At this point, we will stop our hacking tutorial, because the next step
would likely constitute a felony. However, the main point should be apparent: it's really easy to start hacking websites! Metasploit and Kali Linux are
used by real-world hackers and can be set up in a few minutes. They don't
require any particular expertise to use, yet they are phenomenally good at
identifying vulnerabilities in websites and exploiting them.

    This is the reality we are dealing with as web developers today. The
websites we build are available to anyone with an internet connection, as
are the hacking tools that can be used to target them. Don't panic, though!
By the end of the book, you will (hopefully) know as much about security
as the hackers themselves, and be fully prepared for when they attack your
site. So, let's get started by discussing the building blocks of the internet
protocol suite.

PART I

THE BASICS

2

HOW THE INTERNET WORKS

 To become an expert on web security, you need a firm grasp of the internet's underlying web technologies and protocols. This chapter examines the Internet Protocol Suite, which dictates how computers exchange data over the web. You'll also learn about stateful connections and encryption, which are key elements of the modern web. I'll highlight where security holes tend to appear along the way.

The Internet Protocol Suite

In the early days of the internet, data exchange wasn't reliable. The first message sent over the *Advanced Research Projects Agency Network (ARPANET)*, the predecessor to the internet, was a LOGIN command destined for a remote computer at Stanford University. The network sent the first two letters, LO, and then crashed. This was a problem for the US military, which was looking for a way to connect remote computers so that they could continue to exchange information even if a Soviet nuclear strike took various parts of the network offline.

To address this problem, the network engineers developed the *Transmission Control Protocol (TCP)* to ensure a reliable exchange of information between computers. TCP is one of about 20 network protocols that are collectively referred to as the *internet protocol suite*. When a computer sends a message to another machine via TCP, the message is split into data packets that are sent toward their eventual destination with a destination address. The computers that make up the internet push each packet toward the destination without having to process the whole message.

Once the recipient computer receives the packets, it assembles them back into a usable order according to the *sequence number* on each packet. Every time the recipient receives a packet, it sends a receipt. If the recipient fails to acknowledge receipt of a packet, the sender resends that packet, possibly along a different network path. In this way, TCP allows computers to deliver data across a network that is expected to be unreliable.

TCP has undergone significant improvements as the internet has grown. Packets are now sent with a *checksum* that allows recipients to detect data corruption and determine whether packets need to be resent. Senders also preemptively adjust the rate at which they send data according to how fast it's being consumed. (Internet servers are usually magnitudes more powerful than the clients that receive their messages, so they need to be careful not to overwhelm the client's capacity.)

NOTE *TCP remains the most common protocol because of its delivery guarantees, but nowadays, several other protocols are also used over the internet. The* User Datagram Protocol (UDP), *for instance, is a newer protocol that deliberately allows packets to be dropped so that data can be streamed at a constant rate. UDP is commonly used for streaming live video, since consumers prefer a few dropped frames over having their feed delayed when the network gets congested.*

Internet Protocol Addresses

Data packets on the internet are sent to *Internet Protocol (IP) addresses*, numbers assigned to individual internet-connected computers. Each IP address must be unique, so new IP addresses are issued in a structured fashion.

At the highest level, the *Internet Corporation for Assigned Names and Numbers (ICANN)* allots blocks of IP addresses to regional authorities. These regional authorities then grant the blocks of addresses to *internet service providers (ISPs)* and hosting companies within their region. When you connect your browser to the internet, your ISP assigns your computer an IP address that stays fixed for a few months. (ISPs tend to rotate IP addresses for clients periodically.) Similarly, companies that host content on the internet are assigned an IP address for each server they connect to the network.

IP addresses are binary numbers, generally written in *IP version 4 (IPv4)* syntax, which allows for 2^{32} (4,294,967,296) addresses. Google's domain name server, for instance, has the address 8.8.8.8. Because IPv4 addresses are getting used up at a rate that isn't sustainable, the internet is shifting to *IP version 6 (IPv6)* addresses to allow for more connected devices, represented as eight groups of four hexadecimal digits separated by colons (for example: 2001:0db8:0000:0042:0000:8a2e:0370:7334).

The Domain Name System

Browsers and other internet-connected software can recognize and route traffic to IP addresses, but IP addresses aren't particularly memorable for humans. To make website addresses friendlier to users, we use a global directory called the *Domain Name System (DNS)* to translate human-readable *domains* like *example.com* to IP addresses like 93.184.216.119. Domain names are simply placeholders for IP addresses. Domain names, like IP addresses, are unique, and have to be registered before use with private organizations called *domain registrars*.

When browsers encounter a domain name for the first time, they use a local *domain name server* (typically hosted by an ISP) to look it up, and then cache the result to prevent time-consuming lookups in the future. This caching behavior means that new domains or changes to existing domains take a while to propagate on the internet. Exactly how long this propagation takes is controlled by the *time-to-live (TTL)* variable, which is set on the DNS record and instructs DNS caches when to expire the record. DNS caching enables a type of attack called *DNS poisoning*, whereby a local DNS cache is deliberately corrupted so that data is routed to a server controlled by an attacker.

In addition to returning IP addresses for particular domains, domain name servers host records that can describe domain aliases via *canonical name (CNAME) records* that allow multiple domain names to point to the same IP address. DNS can also help route email by using *mail exchange (MX)* records. We'll examine how DNS records can help combat unsolicited email (spam) in Chapter 16.

Application Layer Protocols

TCP allows two computers to reliably exchange data on the internet, but it doesn't dictate how the data being sent should be interpreted. For that to happen, both computers need to agree to exchange information through another, higher-level protocol in the suite. Protocols that build on top of TCP (or UDP) are called *application layer protocols*. Figure 2-1 illustrates how application layer protocols sit above TCP in the internet protocol suite.

The lower-level protocols of the internet protocol suite provide basic data routing over a network, while the higher-level protocols in the application layer provide more structure for applications exchanging data. Many types of applications use TCP as a transport mechanism on the internet.

For example, emails are sent using the Simple Mail Transport Protocol (SMTP), instant messaging software often uses the Extensible Messaging and Presence Protocol (XMPP), file servers make downloads available via the File Transfer Protocol (FTP), and web servers use the HyperText Transfer Protocol (HTTP). Because the web is our chief focus, let's look at HTTP in more detail.

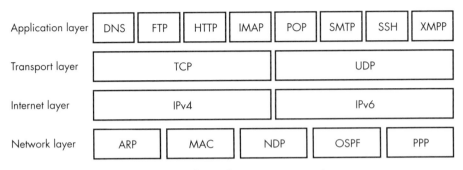

Figure 2-1: The various layers that make up the internet protocol suite

HyperText Transfer Protocol

Web servers use the *HyperText Transfer Protocol (HTTP)* to transport web pages and their resources to *user agents* such as web browsers. In an HTTP conversation, the user agent generates *requests* for particular resources. Web servers, expecting these requests, return *responses* containing either the requested resource, or an error code if the request can't be fulfilled. Both HTTP requests and responses are plaintext messages, though they're often sent in compressed and encrypted form. All of the exploits described in this book use HTTP in some fashion, so it's worth knowing how the requests and responses that make up HTTP conversations work in detail.

HTTP Requests

An HTTP request sent by a browser consists of the following elements:

Method Also known as a *verb*, this describes the action that the user agent wants the server to perform.

Universal resource locator (URL) This describes the resource being manipulated or fetched.

Headers These supply metadata such as the type of content the user agent is expecting or whether it accepts compressed responses.

Body This optional component contains any extra data that needs to be sent to the server.

Listing 2-1 shows an HTTP request.

```
GET❶ http://example.com/❷
❸ User-Agent: Mozilla/5.0 (Macintosh; Intel Mac OS X 10_13_6)
  AppleWebKit/537.36 (KHTML, like Gecko) Chrome/67.0.3396.99 Safari/537.36
❹ Accept: text/html,application/xhtml+xml,application/xml; */*
```

```
Accept-Encoding: gzip, deflate
Accept-Language: en-GB,en-US;q=0.9,en;q=0.8
```

Listing 2-1: A simple HTTP request

The method ❶ and the URL ❷ appear on the first line. These are followed by HTTP headers on separate lines. The User-Agent header ❸ tells the website the type of browser that is making the request. The Accept header ❹ tells the website the type of content the browser is expecting.

Requests that use the GET method—called GET requests for short—are the most common type of request on the internet. GET requests fetch a particular resource on the web server, identified by a specific URL. The response to a GET request will contain a resource: perhaps a web page, an image, or even the results of a search request. The example request in Listing 2-1 represents an attempt to load the home page of *example.com*, and would be generated when a user types *example.com* in the browser's navigation bar.

If the browser needs to send information to the server, rather than just fetch data, it typically uses a POST request. When you fill out a form on a web page and submit it, the browser sends a POST request. Because POST requests contain information sent to the server, the browser sends that information in a *request body*, after the HTTP headers.

In Chapter 8, you'll see why it's important to use POST rather than GET requests when sending data to your server. Websites that erroneously use GET requests for doing anything other than retrieving resources are vulnerable to cross-site request forgery attacks.

When writing a website, you may also encounter PUT, PATCH, and DELETE requests. These are used to upload, edit, or delete resources on the server, respectively, and are typically triggered by JavaScript embedded in a web page. Table 2-1 documents a handful of other methods that are worth knowing about.

Table 2-1: The Lesser-Known HTTP Methods

HTTP method	Function and implementation
HEAD	A HEAD request retrieves the same information as a GET request, but instructs the server to return the response without a body (in other words, the useful part). If you implement a GET method on your web server, the server will generally respond to HEAD requests automatically.
CONNECT	CONNECT initiates two-way communications. You'll use it in your HTTP client code if you ever have to connect through a proxy.
OPTIONS	Sending an OPTIONS request lets a user agent ask what other methods are supported by a resource. Your web server will generally respond to OPTIONS requests by inferring which other methods you have implemented.
TRACE	A response to a TRACE request will contain an exact copy of the original HTTP request, so the client can see what (if any) alterations were made by intermediate servers. This sounds useful, but it's generally recommended that you turn off TRACE requests in your web server, because they can act as a security hole. For instance, they can allow malicious JavaScript injected into a page to access cookies that have been deliberately made inaccessible to JavaScript.

Once a web server receives an HTTP request, it replies to the user agent with an HTTP response. Let's break down how responses are structured.

HTTP Responses

HTTP responses sent back by a web server begin with a protocol description, a three-digit *status code*, and, typically, a *status message* that indicates whether the request can be fulfilled. The response also contains headers providing metadata that instructs the browser how to treat the content. Finally, most responses contain a body that itself contains the requested resource. Listing 2-2 shows the contents of a simple HTTP response.

```
HTTP/1.1❶ 200❷ OK❸
❹ Content-Encoding: gzip
  Accept-Ranges: bytes
  Cache-Control: max-age=604800
  Content-Type: text/html
  Content-Length: 606

❺ <!doctype html>
  <html>
     <head>
        <title>Example Domain</title>
   ❻ <style type="text/css">
           body {
              background-color: #f0f0f2;
              font-family: "Open Sans", "Helvetica Neue", Helvetica, sans-serif;
           }
           div {
              width: 600px;
              padding: 50px;
              background-color: #fff;
              border-radius: 1em;
           }
        </style>
     </head>
  ❼ <body>
        <div>
           <h1>Example Domain</h1>
           <p>This domain is established to be used for illustrative examples.</p>
           <p>
              <a href="http://www.iana.org/domains/example">More information...</a>
           </p>
        </div>
     </body>
  </html>
```

Listing 2-2: An HTTP response from example.com, the world's least interesting website

The response begins with the protocol description ❶, the status code ❷, and the status message ❸. Status codes formatted as 2*xx* indicate that the request was understood, accepted, and responded to. Codes formatted as

3xx redirect the client to a different URL. Codes formatted as *4xx* indicate a client error: the browser generated an apparently invalid request. (The most common error of this type is HTTP 404 Not Found). Codes formatted as *5xx* indicate a server error: the request was valid, but the server was unable to fulfill the request.

Next are the HTTP headers ❹. Almost all HTTP responses include a Content-Type header that indicates the kind of data being returned. Responses to GET requests also often contain a Cache-Control header to indicate that the client should cache large resources (for example, images) locally.

If the HTTP response is successful, the body contains the resource the client was trying to access—often *HyperText Markup Language (HTML)* ❺ describing the structure of the requested web page. In this case, the response contains styling information ❻ as well as the page content itself ❼. Other types of responses may return JavaScript code, Cascading Style Sheets (CSS) used for styling HTML, or binary data in the body.

Stateful Connections

Web servers typically deal with many user agents at once, but HTTP does nothing to distinguish which requests are coming from which user agent. This wasn't an important consideration in the early days of the internet, because web pages were largely read-only. Modern websites, however, often allow users to log in and will track their activity as they visit and interact with different pages. To allow for this, HTTP conversations need to be made stateful. A connection or conversation between a client and a server is *stateful* when they perform a "handshake" and continue to send packets back and forth until one of the communicating parties decides to terminate the connection.

When a web server wants to keep track of which user it's responding to with each request, and thus achieve a stateful HTTP conversation, it needs to establish a mechanism to track the user agent as it makes the subsequent requests. The entire conversation between a particular user agent and a web server is called an *HTTP session*. The most common way of tracking sessions is for the server to send back a Set-Cookie header in the initial HTTP response. This asks the user agent receiving the response to store a *cookie*, a small snippet of text data pertaining to that particular web domain. The user agent then returns the same data in the Cookie header of any subsequent HTTP request to the web server. If implemented correctly, the contents of the cookie being passed back and forth uniquely identify the user agent and hence establish the HTTP session.

Session information contained in cookies is a juicy target for hackers. If an attacker steals another user's cookie, they can pretend to be that user on the website. Similarly, if an attacker successfully persuades a website to accept a forged cookie, they can impersonate any user they please. We'll look at various methods of stealing and forging cookies in Chapter 10.

Encryption

When the web was first invented, HTTP requests and responses were sent in plaintext form, which meant they could be read by anyone intercepting the data packets; this kind of interception is known as a *man-in-the-middle attack*. Because private communication and online transactions are common on the modern web, web servers and browsers protect their users from such attacks by using *encryption*, a method of disguising the contents of messages from prying eyes by encoding them during transmission.

To secure their communications, web servers and browsers send requests and responses by using *Transport Layer Security (TLS)*, a method of encryption that provides both privacy and data integrity. TLS ensures that packets intercepted by a third party can't be decrypted without the appropriate encryption keys. It also ensures that any attempt to tamper with the packets will be detectable, which ensures data integrity.

HTTP conversations conducted using TLS are called *HTTP Secure (HTTPS)*. HTTPS requires the client and server to perform a *TLS handshake* in which both parties agree on an encryption method (a cipher) and exchange encryption keys. Once the handshake is complete, any further messages (both requests and responses) will be opaque to outsiders.

Encryption is a complex topic but is key to securing your website. We'll examine how to enable encryption for your website in Chapter 13.

Summary

In this chapter, you learned about the plumbing of the internet. TCP enables reliable communication between internet-connected computers that each have an IP address. The Domain Name System provides human-readable aliases for IP addresses. HTTP builds on top of TCP to send HTTP requests from user agents (such as web browsers) to web servers, which in turn reply with HTTP responses. Each request is sent to a specific URL, and you learned about various types of HTTP methods. Web servers respond with status codes, and send back cookies to initiate stateful connections. Finally, encryption (in the form of HTTPS) can be used to secure communication between a user agent and a web server.

In the next chapter, you'll take a look at what happens when a web browser receives an HTTP response—how a web page is rendered, and how user actions can generate more HTTP requests.

3

HOW BROWSERS WORK

Most internet users interact with websites through a browser. To build secure websites, you need to understand how browsers transform the HyperText Markup Language (HTML) used to describe web pages into the interactive, visual representations you see onscreen. This chapter covers how a modern browser renders a web page, highlighting the security measures it puts in place to protect the user—the *browser security model*. We'll also look at the various ways hackers try to overcome these security measures.

Web Page Rendering

The software component within a web browser that's responsible for transforming a web page's HTML into the visual representation you see onscreen is called the *rendering pipeline*. The rendering pipeline is responsible for parsing the page's HTML, understanding the structure and content of the document, and converting it to a series of drawing operations that the operating system can understand.

For websites in the early days of the internet, this process was relatively simple. Web page HTML contained very little styling information (such as color, font, and font size), so rendering was mostly a matter of loading text and images and drawing them onscreen in the order they appeared in the HTML document. HTML was envisioned as a *markup language*, meaning it described the web page by breaking it into semantic elements and annotating how the information was structured. The early web looked pretty crude, but was very efficient for relaying textual content.

Nowadays, web design is more elaborate and visually appealing. Web developers encode styling information into separate *Cascading Style Sheets (CSS)* files, which instruct the browser precisely how each page element is to be displayed. A modern, hyperoptimized browser like Google Chrome contains several million lines of code to correctly interpret and render HTML and deal with conflicting styling rules in a fast, uniform manner. Understanding the various stages that make up the rendering pipeline will help you appreciate this complexity.

The Rendering Pipeline: An Overview

We'll get into the details of each stage of the rendering pipeline in a moment, but first let's look at the high-level process.

When the browser receives an HTTP response, it parses the HTML in the body of the response into a *Document Object Model (DOM)*: an in-memory data structure that represents the browser's understanding of the way the page is structured. Generating the DOM is an interim step between parsing the HTML and drawing it onscreen. In modern HTML, the layout of the page can't be determined until the whole of the HTML is parsed, because the order of the tags in the HTML doesn't necessarily determine the location of their content.

Once the browser generates the DOM, but before anything can be drawn onscreen, styling rules must be applied to each DOM element. These styling rules declare how each page element is to be drawn—the foreground and background color, the font style and size, the position and alignment, and so on. Last, after the browser finalizes the structure of the page and breaks down how to apply styling information, it draws the web page onscreen. All of this happens in a fraction of a second, and repeats on a loop as the user interacts with the page.

The browser also loads and executes any JavaScript it comes across as it constructs the DOM. JavaScript code can dynamically make changes to the DOM and styling rules, either before the page is rendered or in response to user actions.

Now let's look at each step in more detail.

The Document Object Model

When a browser first receives an HTTP response containing HTML, it parses the HTML document into a DOM, a data structure describing the HTML document as a series of nested elements called *DOM nodes*. Some nodes in the DOM correspond to elements to be rendered onscreen, such as input boxes and paragraphs of text; other nodes, such as script and styling elements, control the page's behavior and layout.

Each DOM node is roughly equivalent to a tag in the original HTML document. DOM nodes can contain text content, or contain other DOM nodes, similar to the way HTML tags can be nested within each other. Because each node can contain other nodes in a branching fashion, web developers talk about the *DOM tree*.

Some HTML tags, like the `<script>`, `<style>`, `<image>`, `<font>`, and `<video>` tags, can reference an external URL in an attribute. When they're parsed into the DOM, these tags cause the browser to import the external resources, meaning that the browser must initiate a further HTTP request. Modern browsers perform these requests in parallel to the page rendering, in order to speed up the page-load time.

The construction of the DOM from HTML is designed to be as robust as possible. Browsers are forgiving about malformed HTML; they close unclosed tags, insert missing tags, and ignore corrupted tags as needed. Browser vendors don't punish the web user for the website's errors.

Styling Information

Once the browser has constructed the DOM tree, it needs to determine which DOM nodes correspond to onscreen elements, how to lay out those elements relative to each other, and what styling information to apply to them. Though these styling rules can be defined inline in the HTML document, web developers prefer to encode styling information in separate CSS files. Separating the styling information from the HTML content makes restyling existing content easier and keeps HTML content as clean and semantic as possible. It also makes HTML easier to parse for alternative browsing technologies such as screen readers.

When using CSS, a web developer will create one or more *stylesheets* to declare how elements on the page should be rendered. The HTML document will import these stylesheets by using a `<style>` tag referencing the external URL that hosts the stylesheet. Each stylesheet contains *selectors* that pick out tags in the HTML document and assign styling information, such as font size, colors, and position, to each. Selectors may be simple: they might state, for example, that heading text in an `<h1>` tag should be rendered in blue. For more complex web pages, selectors get more convoluted: a selector may describe how quickly a hyperlink changes color when the user moves their mouse over it.

The rendering pipeline implements a lot of logic to decipher final styling, because strict rules of precedence need to be followed about how styles are applied. Each selector can apply to multiple page elements, and each page element will often have styling information supplied by several selectors. One of the growing pains of the early internet was figuring out how to create a website that looked the same when rendered by different types of browsers. Modern browsers are generally consistent in the way they render a web page, but they still vary. The industry's benchmark for compliance to web standards is the Acid3 test, as shown in Figure 3-1. Only a few browsers score 100. You can visit *http://acid3.acidtests.org/* to try out the Acid3 test.

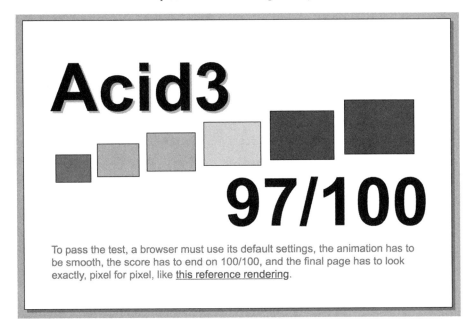

Figure 3-1: Acid3, making sure browsers can render colored rectangles correctly since 2008

The construction of the DOM tree and the application of styling rules occur in parallel to the processing of any JavaScript code contained in the web page. This JavaScript code can change the structure and layout of the page even before it's rendered, so let's take a quick look at how the execution of JavaScript dovetails with the rendering pipeline.

JavaScript

Modern web pages use JavaScript to respond to user actions. *JavaScript* is a fully fledged programming language that is executed by the browser's JavaScript engine when web pages are rendered. JavaScript can be incorporated into an HTML document by using a <script> tag; the code may be included inline within the HTML document, or, more typically, the <script> tag will reference a JavaScript file that is to be loaded from an external URL.

By default, any JavaScript code is executed by the browser as soon as the relevant <script> tag is parsed into a DOM node. For JavaScript code loaded from an external URL, this means the code is executed as soon as it is loaded.

This default behavior causes problems if the rendering pipeline hasn't finished parsing the HTML document; the JavaScript code will attempt to interact with page elements that may not yet exist in the DOM. To allow for this, <script> tags are often marked with a defer attribute. This causes the JavaScript to execute only when the entire DOM has been constructed.

As you would imagine, the fact that browsers eagerly execute any JavaScript code they come across has security implications. A hacker's end goal is often the remote execution of code on another user's machine, and the internet makes this goal much easier, as it's rare to find a computer that isn't connected to the network in some way. For this reason, modern browsers heavily restrict JavaScript with the *browser security model*. This dictates that JavaScript code must be executed within a *sandbox*, where it's *not* permitted to perform any of the following actions:

- Start new processes or access other existing processes.
- Read arbitrary chunks of system memory. As a *managed memory language*, JavaScript can't read memory outside its sandbox.
- Access the local disk. Modern browsers allow websites to store small amounts of data locally, but this storage is abstracted from the filesystem itself.
- Access the operating system's network layer.
- Call operating system functions.

JavaScript executing in the browser sandbox *is* permitted to do the following actions:

- Read and manipulate the DOM of the current web page.
- Listen to and respond to user actions on the current page by registering event listeners.
- Make HTTP calls on behalf of the user.
- Open new web pages or refresh the URL of the current page, but only in response to a user action.
- Write new entries to the browser history and go backward and forward in history.
- Ask for the user's location. For example, "Google Maps would like to use your location."
- Ask permission to send desktop notifications.

Even with these restrictions, an attacker who can inject malicious Java Script into your web page can still do a lot of harm by using cross-site scripting to read credit card details or credentials as a user enters them. Even tiny amounts of injected JavaScript pose a threat, because injected code can add <script> tags in the DOM to load a malicious payload. We'll look at how to protect against this type of cross-site scripting attack in Chapter 7.

Before and After Rendering: Everything Else the Browser Does

A browser is much more than a rendering pipeline and a JavaScript engine. In addition to rendering HTML and executing JavaScript, modern browsers contain logic for many other responsibilities. Browsers connect with the operating system to resolve and cache DNS addresses, interpret and verify security certificates, encode requests in HTTPS if needed, and store and transmit cookies according to the web server's instructions. To understand how these responsibilities fit together, let's take a behind-the-scenes look at a user logging into Amazon:

1. The user visits *www.amazon.com* in their favorite browser.

2. The browser attempts to resolve the domain (*amazon.com*) to an IP address. First, the browser consults the operating system's DNS cache. If it finds no results, it asks the internet service provider to look in the provider's DNS cache. In the unlikely event that nobody on the ISP has visited the Amazon website before, the ISP will resolve the domain at an authoritative DNS server.

3. Now that it has resolved the IP address, the browser attempts to initiate a TCP handshake with the server corresponding to the IP address in order to establish a secure connection.

4. Once the TCP session has been established, the browser constructs an HTTP GET request to *www.amazon.com*. TCP splits the HTTP request into packets and sends them to the server to be reassembled.

5. At this point, the HTTP conversation upgrades to HTTPS to ensure secure communication. The browser and server undertake a TLS handshake, agree on an encryption cypher, and exchange encryption keys.

6. The server uses the secure channel to send back an HTTP response containing HTML of the Amazon front page. The browser parses and displays the page, typically triggering many other HTTP GET requests.

7. The user navigates to the login page, enters their login credentials, and submits the login form, which generates a POST request to the server.

8. The server validates the login credentials and establishes a session by returning a Set-Cookie header in the response. The browser stores the cookie for the prescribed time, and sends it back with subsequent requests to Amazon.

    After all of this happens, the user can access their Amazon account.

Summary

This chapter reviewed how browsers transform the HTML used to describe web pages into the interactive, visual representations you see onscreen. The browser's rendering pipeline parses HTML documents into a Document Object Model (DOM), applies styling information from Cascading Style Sheets (CSS) files, and then lays out the DOM nodes onscreen.

You also learned about the browser security model. The browser executes JavaScript included in <script> tags under strict security rules. You also reviewed a simple HTTP conversation illustrating the browser's many other responsibilities beyond rendering pages: reconstructing HTTP from TCP packets, verifying security certificates and securing communication using HTTPS, and storing and transmitting cookies.

In the next chapter, you'll look at the other end of the HTTP conversation: the web server.

4

HOW WEB SERVERS WORK

In the previous chapter, you learned how browsers communicate over the internet and render the HTML pages and other resources that make up a website. In this chapter, you'll learn about how those same HTML pages are constructed by web servers.

By its simplest definition, a *web server* is a computer program that sends back HTML pages in response to HTTP requests. Modern web servers encompass a much broader range of functionality than this suggests, however. When a browser makes an HTTP request, modern web servers allow code to be executed in order to generate the web page HTML dynamically, and often incorporate content from a database. As a web developer, you'll spend most of your time writing and testing this type of code.

This chapter covers how developers organize code and resources within a web server. I'll also pinpoint common weaknesses in web servers that allow security vulnerabilities to occur, and talk about how to avoid these pitfalls.

Static and Dynamic Resources

Web servers serve two types of content in response to HTTP requests: static resources and dynamic resources. A *static resource* is an HTML file, image file, or other type of file that the web server returns unaltered in HTTP responses. A *dynamic resource* is code, a script, or a template that the web server executes or interprets in response to an HTTP request. Modern web servers are capable of hosting both static and dynamic resources. Which resource the server executes or returns depends on the URL in the HTTP request. Your web server will resolve URLs according to a configuration file that maps URL patterns to particular resources.

Let's look at how web servers handle static and dynamic resources.

Static Resources

In the early days of the internet, websites consisted mostly of static resources. Developers coded HTML files by hand, and websites consisted of individual HTML files that were deployed to the web server. The "deployment" of a website required the developer to copy all the HTML files to the web server and restart the server process. When a user wished to visit the website, they would type the website's URL in their browser. The browser would make an HTTP request to the web server hosting the website, which would interpret the incoming URL as a request for a file on disk. Finally, the web server would return the HTML file as is in the HTTP response.

An example of this is the website for the 1996 movie *Space Jam*. It consists entirely of static resources, and it's still online at *spacejam.com*. Clicking through the site takes us back to a simpler and aesthetically less sophisticated time in web development. If you visit the website, you will notice that each of the URLs like *https://www.spacejam.com/cmp/sitemap.html* end with a *.html* suffix, indicating that each web page corresponds to an HTML file on the server.

Tim Berners-Lee's original vision of the web looked much like the *Space Jam* website: a network of static files hosted on web servers that would contain all the world's information.

URL Resolution

Modern web servers handle static resources in much the same way as their older counterparts. To access a resource in a browser, you include the resource name in the URL, and the web server returns the resource file from disk as it's requested. To display the picture shown in Figure 4-1, the URL includes the resource name */images/hedgehog_in_spaghetti.png*, and the web server returns the appropriate file from disk.

Figure 4-1: An example of a static resource

Modern web servers have a few additional tricks up their sleeves. A modern web server allows any URL to be mapped to a particular static resource. We would expect the *hedgehog_in_spaghetti.png* resource to be a file living in the */images* directory on the web server, but in fact, the developer can call it anything they choose. By unlinking the URL from the filepath, web servers give developers more freedom to organize their code. This might allow each user to have a different profile image, but use the same path, for instance.

When returning a static resource, modern web servers often add data to the HTTP response or process the static resource before returning it. For example, web servers often dynamically compress large resource files by using the gzip algorithm to reduce the bandwidth used in the response, or add caching headers in HTTP responses to instruct the browser to cache and use a local copy of a static resource if a user views it again within a defined window of time. This makes the website more responsive for the user and reduces the load the server has to handle.

Because static resources are simply files of one form or another, they don't, by themselves, exhibit much in the way of security vulnerabilities. The process of resolving a URL to a file *can* introduce vulnerabilities, however. If a user designates certain types of files to be private (for example, the images they upload), you will need to have *access control* rules defined on the web server. We'll look at various ways hackers attempt to circumvent access control rules in Chapter 11.

Content Delivery Networks

A modern innovation designed to improve the delivery speeds of static files is the *content delivery network (CDN)*, which will store duplicated copies of static resources in data centers around the world, and quickly deliver those resources to browsers from the nearest physical location. CDNs like Cloudflare, Akamai, or Amazon CloudFront offload the burden of serving large resource files, such as images, to a third party. As such, they allow even small companies to produce responsive websites without a massive server expenditure. Integrating a CDN into your site is usually straightforward, and the CDN service charges a monthly fee depending on the amount of resources you deploy.

Using a CDN also introduces security complications. Integrating with a CDN effectively allows a third party to serve content under your security certificate, so you need to set up your CDN integration securely. We'll investigate how to securely integrate third-party services such as CDNs in Chapter 14.

Content Management Systems

Plenty of websites still consist of mostly static content. Rather than being coded by hand, these sites are generally built using *content management systems (CMSs)* that provide authoring tools requiring little to no technical knowledge to write the content. CMSs generally impose a uniform style on the pages and allow administrators to update content directly in the browser.

CMS plug-ins can also provide analytics to track visitors, add appointment management or customer support functions, and even create online stores. This plug-in approach is part of a larger trend of websites using specialized services from third-party companies to build custom features. For example, sites commonly use Google Analytics for customer tracking, Facebook Login for authentication, and Zendesk for customer support. You can add each of these features with a few lines of code and an API key, making it significantly easier to build feature-rich sites from scratch.

Using other people's code to build your site, either by integrating a CMS or using plug-in services, theoretically makes you more secure because these third parties employ security professionals and have an incentive to secure their services. However, the ubiquity of these services and plug-ins also makes them a target for hackers. For example, many self-hosted instances of WordPress, the most popular CMS, are infrequently patched. You can easily discover WordPress vulnerabilities through a simple Google search, as shown in Figure 4-2.

When you use third-party code, you need to stay on top of security advisories and deploy security patches as soon as they become available. We'll investigate some of risks around third-party code and services in Chapter 14.

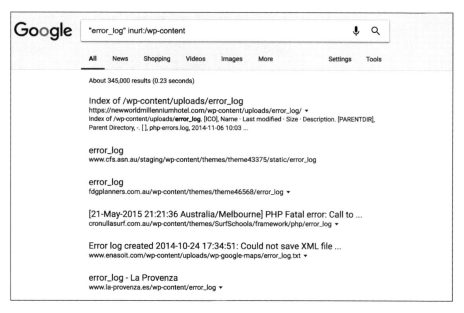

Figure 4-2: Come get your unsecured WordPress instances.

Dynamic Resources

Though it's simpler to use static resources, authoring individual HTML files by hand is time-consuming. Imagine if retail websites had to code up a new web page every time they added a new item to their inventory. It would inefficiently use up everyone's time (though it would provide a guarantee of job security for web developers).

Most modern websites instead use dynamic resources. Often the dynamic resource's code loads data from a database in order to populate the HTTP response. Typically, the dynamic resource outputs HTML, though other content types can be returned depending on the expectations of the browser.

Dynamic resources allow retail websites to implement a single product web page capable of displaying many types of products. Each time a user views a particular product on the site, the web page extracts the product code from a URL, loads the product price, image, and description from the database, and interpolates this data into the HTML. Adding new products to the retailer's inventory then becomes a matter of simply entering new rows in the database.

There are many other uses for dynamic resources. If you access your banking website, it looks up your account details and incorporates them in the HTML. A search engine like Google returns matches pulled from Google's massive search index and returns them in a dynamic page. Many sites, including social media and web-mail sites, look different to each user, because they dynamically construct the HTML after the user logs in.

As useful as dynamic resources are, they create novel security vulnerabilities. The dynamic interpolation of content into the HTML can be vulnerable to attack. We'll look at how to protect ourselves from maliciously injected JavaScript in Chapter 7, and see how HTTP requests generated from other websites can cause harm in Chapter 8.

Templates

The first dynamic resources were simple script files, often written in the Perl language, that the web server executed when a user visited a particular URL. These script files would write out the HTML that made up a particular web page.

Code that makes up a dynamic resource in this fashion often isn't intuitive to read. If a web page consists of static resources, you can look at a static HTML file to get a sense of how it's organized, but it's harder to do the same with dynamic resources that have a thousand lines of Perl code. Essentially, you have one language (Perl) writing out content in another language (HTML) that, downstream, a browser will render onscreen. Making changes to Perl code while keeping in mind what the eventual rendered output will look like is a difficult task.

To address this, web developers often use template files to build dynamic web pages. *Templates* are mostly HTML, but have programmatic logic interspersed within them that contains instructions to the web server. This logic is generally simple and usually does one of three things: pull data from a database or the HTTP request and interpolate it into the HTML, conditionally render sections of the HTML template, or loop over a data structure (for example, lists of items) to repeatedly render a block of HTML. All modern web frameworks use template files (with variations in syntax) because inserting code snippets into HTML typically makes code cleaner and more readable.

Databases

When a web server executes the code in a dynamic resource, it often loads data from a database. If you visit a retail website, the web server looks up the product ID in a database, and uses the product information stored in the database to construct the page. If you log into a social media site, the web server loads your timeline and notifications from an underlying database in order to write the HTML. In fact, most modern websites use databases to store user information, and the interface between the web server and a database is a frequent target for hackers.

Database technology predates the invention of the web. As computers became more widespread back in the 1960s, companies started to see the value of digitizing and centralizing their record keeping to make searching and maintenance easier. With the birth of the web, sticking a web frontend on top of a product inventory database was a natural progression for companies looking to branch out into online retail.

Databases are key for authentication too. If a website wants to identify returning users, it needs to keep a record of who has signed up to the site and verify, or *authenticate*, their login information against stored credentials when they return.

The two most commonly used types of databases are SQL and NoSQL. Let's take a look at both.

SQL Databases

The most common databases used today are relational databases that implement *Structured Query Language (SQL)*, a declarative programming language that maintains and fetches data.

SQL can be pronounced either "ess-qew-ell" or "sequel," although you can try pronouncing it "squeal" if you want to see your database administrator squirm uncomfortably.

SQL databases are *relational*, which means they store data in one or more *tables* that relate to each other in formally prescribed ways. You can think of a table as akin to a Microsoft Excel spreadsheet with rows and columns, with each row representing a data item, and each column representing a data point for each item. Columns in a SQL database have predefined data types, typically strings of text (often of fixed length), numbers, or dates.

Database tables in a relational database relate to each other via *keys*. Usually, each row in a table has a unique numeric *primary key*, and tables can refer to each other's rows via *foreign keys*. For example, if you were storing user orders as database records, the orders table would have a foreign key column called user_id that represents the user who placed the order. Instead of storing user information directly in the orders table, this user_id column would contain foreign-key values that refer to a specific row's primary key (the id column) in the users table. This type of relation ensures that you cannot store orders in the database without storing the user, and ensures that only a single source of truth exists for each user.

Relational databases also feature *data integrity constraints* that prevent data corruption and make uniform queries to the database possible. Like foreign keys, other types of data integrity constraints can be defined in SQL. For example, you could require the email_address column in a users table to contain only unique values, to force each user in the database to have a different email address. You could also require non-null values in tables so that the database must specify an email address for each user.

SQL databases also exhibit transactional and consistent behavior. A database *transaction* is a group of SQL statements executed in a batch. A database is said to be *transactional* if each transaction is "all or nothing": that is, if any SQL statement fails to execute within the batch, the entire transaction fails and leaves the database state unchanged. SQL databases are *consistent* because any successful transaction brings the database from one valid state to another. Any attempt to insert invalid data in a SQL database causes the whole transaction to fail and the database to remain unaltered.

Because data stored in SQL databases is often highly sensitive, hackers target databases to sell their contents on the black market. Hackers also often take advantage of insecurely constructed SQL statements. We'll examine how in Chapter 6.

NoSQL Databases

SQL databases are often the bottleneck of a web application's performance. If most HTTP requests hitting a website generate a database call, the database server will experience a tremendous load and slow the performance of the website for all users.

These performance concerns have led to the increasing popularity of NoSQL databases—databases that sacrifice the strict data integrity requirements of traditional SQL databases to achieve greater scalability. NoSQL encompasses a variety of approaches to storing and accessing data, but a few trends among them have emerged.

NoSQL databases are often *schemaless*, allowing you to add fields to new records without having to upgrade any data structures. To achieve this flexibility, data is often stored in *key-value* form, or in *JavaScript Object Notation (JSON)*.

NoSQL database technology also tends to prioritize widescale replication of data over absolute consistency. SQL databases guarantee that simultaneous queries by different client programs will see the same results; NoSQL databases often loosen this constraint and guarantee only *eventual consistency*.

NoSQL databases make storing unstructured or semistructured data very easy. Extracting and querying data tends to be a little more complex— some databases offer a programmatic interface, while others implement their own query languages that adapt SQL-like syntax to their data structures. NoSQL databases are vulnerable to injection attacks in much the same way as SQL databases are, though an attacker has to correctly guess the database type to successfully mount an attack.

Distributed Caches

Dynamic resources can also load data from in-memory distributed *caches*, another popular approach to achieving the massive scalability required by large websites. *Caching* refers to the process of storing a copy of data kept elsewhere in an easily retrievable form, to speed up retrieval of that data. *Distributed caches* like Redis or Memcached make caching data straightforward and allow software to share data structures across different servers and processes in a language-agnostic way. Distributed caches can be shared among web servers, making them ideal for storing frequently accessed data that would otherwise have to be retrieved from a database.

Large web companies typically implement their tech stacks as a range of *microservices*—simple, modular services that perform one action on demand—and use distributed caches to communicate between them. Services often communicate via *queues* stored in a distributed cache: data structures that can put tasks in a waiting state so they can be completed one at a time by numerous worker processes. Services can also use *publish-subscribe* channels that allow many processes to register interest in a type of event, and have them notified en masse when it occurs.

Distributed caches are vulnerable to hacks in the same way that databases are. Thankfully, Redis and Memcached were developed in an age when these kinds of threats were well-known, so best practices are generally baked into *software development kits (SDKs)*, the code libraries you use to connect with the caches.

Web Programming Languages

Web servers will execute code in the process of evaluating dynamic resources. A huge number of programming languages can be used to write web server code, and each has different security considerations.

Let's look at some of the more commonly used languages. We'll use these languages in code samples in later chapters.

Ruby (on Rails)

The *Ruby* programming language, like *Dragon Ball Z* and the Tom Selleck film *Mr. Baseball*, was invented in Japan in the mid '90s. Unlike either *Dragon Ball Z* or Tom Selleck, it didn't become popular for another decade until the Ruby on Rails platform was released.

Ruby on Rails incorporates many best practices for building large-scale web applications and makes them easy to implement with minimal configuration. The Rails community also takes security seriously. Rails was one of the first web server stacks to incorporate protections against cross-site request forgery attacks. Nevertheless, Rail's ubiquity makes it a common target for hackers. Several major security vulnerabilities have been discovered (and hastily patched) in recent years.

Simpler Ruby web servers often described as *microframeworks* (for example, *Sinatra*) have become popular alternatives to Rails in recent years. Microframeworks allow you to combine individual code libraries that perform one particular function, so your web server is deliberately minimal in size. This contrasts with Rails's "everything including the kitchen sink" model of deployment. Developers who use a microframework generally find the extra capabilities they need by using the RubyGems package manager.

Python

The *Python* language was invented in the late 1980s. Its clean syntax, flexible programming paradigm, and wide variety of modules have made the language phenomenally popular. Newcomers to Python are often surprised that whitespace and indenting have semantic meaning, which is unusual among programming languages. Whitespace is so important in the Python community that they fight holy wars over whether indentation should be done with tabs or spaces.

Python is used for a variety of applications, and is often the go-to language for data science and scientific computing projects. Web developers have a wide choice of actively maintained web servers to choose from (such as the popular Django and Flask). The diversity of web servers also acts as a security feature because hackers are less likely to target a particular platform.

JavaScript and Node.js

JavaScript started out as a simple language for executing small scripts within the browser, but became popular for writing web server code and rapidly evolved with the *Node.js* runtime. Node.js runs on top of the V8 JavaScript *engine*, the same software component that Google Chrome uses to interpret JavaScript within the browser. JavaScript still contains many quirks, but the prospect of using the same language on the client side and server side has made Node the fastest-growing web development platform.

The largest security risks in Node are due to its rapid growth—hundreds of modules are added every day. You'll need to take extra caution when you use third-party code in your Node application.

PHP

The *PHP* language was developed from a set of C binaries used to build dynamic sites on Linux. PHP later developed into a fully fledged programming language, though the unplanned evolution of the language is evident in its disorganized nature. PHP inconsistently implements many built-in functions. For example, variable names are case-sensitive, but function names are not. Despite these quirks, PHP remains popular and, at one point, it powered 10 percent of sites on the web.

If you're writing PHP, you're often maintaining a legacy system. Because older PHP frameworks exhibit some of the nastiest security vulnerabilities you can imagine, you should update legacy PHP systems to use modern libraries. Every type of vulnerability, whether it's command execution, directory traversal, or a buffer overflow, has given PHP programmers sleepless nights.

Java

Java and the *Java Virtual Machine (JVM)* have been widely used and implemented in the enterprise space, allowing you to run Java's compiled bytecode across multiple operating systems. It's generally a good workhorse language when performance is a concern.

Developers have used Java for everything, whether for robotics, mobile app development, big-data applications, or embedded devices. Its popularity as a web development language has waned, but many millions of lines of Java code still power the internet. From a security perspective, Java is haunted by its past popularity; legacy applications contain a lot of Java code that run older versions of the language and frameworks. Java developers need to update to secure versions in a timely fashion lest they become easy pickings for hackers.

If you're a more adventurous developer, you'll find other popular languages that run on the JVM and offer compatibility with Java's huge ecosystem of third-party libraries. Clojure is a popular Lisp dialect; Scala is a functional language with static typing; Kotlin is a newer object-oriented language designed to be backward compatible with Java, while making scripting easier.

C#

C# was designed by Microsoft as part of the .NET initiative. C# (and other .NET languages, such as VB.NET) use a virtual machine called the *Common Language Runtime (CLR)*. C# is less abstracted from the operating system than Java, and you can happily intermingle C++ code with C#.

Microsoft has had a conversion late in life to open source evangelism, and the reference implementation of C# is now, thankfully, open source. The Mono project allows .NET applications to run on Linux and other operating systems. Nevertheless, most companies using C# deploy to Windows servers and the typical Microsoft stack. Windows has had a troubling history security-wise—being, for instance, *the* most common target platform for viruses—so anyone looking to adopt .NET as a platform needs to be aware of the risks.

Client-Side JavaScript

As a web developer, you have a choice of languages for writing web server code. But when your code needs to be executed in the browser, you have exactly one choice: JavaScript. As I mentioned previously, the popularity of JavaScript as a server-side language can in part be credited to web developers' familiarity with it from writing for the client side.

JavaScript in the browser has moved a long way beyond the simple form-validation logic and animated widgets it was used for in the early days of the web. A complex site such as Facebook uses JavaScript to redraw areas of the page as the user interacts with it—for example, rendering a menu when the user clicks an icon, or opening a dialog when they click a photo. Sites often update the user interface when background events occur, too, by adding notification markers when others leave comments or write new posts.

Achieving this kind of dynamic user interface without refreshing the whole page and interrupting the user experience requires client-side JavaScript to manage a lot of state in memory. Several frameworks have been developed to organize memory state and render pages efficiently. They also allow for modular reuse of JavaScript code over various pages on the site, a key design consideration when you have millions of lines of JavaScript to manage.

One such JavaScript framework is *Angular,* originally released by Google under an open source license. Angular borrows from server-side paradigms and uses client-side templates to render web pages. The Angular template engine—which executes in the browser as the page loads—parses the template HTML supplied by the server, and processes any directives as they appear. Because the template engine is simply JavaScript executing in the browser, it can write directly to the DOM and short-circuit some of the browser-rendering pipeline. As the memory state changes, Angular automatically re-renders the DOM. This separation makes for cleaner code and more-maintainable web applications.

The open source *React* framework, which was released by the Facebook development team, takes a slightly different approach from Angular. Instead of interspersing code in HTML templates, React encourages the developer to write HTML-like tags directly into JavaScript. React developers typically create *JavaScript XML (JSX)* files that they run through a preprocessor and compile into JavaScript before sending them to the browser.

Writing JavaScript code like `return <h1>Hello, {format(user)}</h1>` for the first time can seem strange to developers used to separating JavaScript and HTML files, but by making HTML a first-class element of the JavaScript syntax, React enables useful features (for example, syntax highlighting and code completion) that would otherwise be difficult to support.

Rich, client-side JavaScript frameworks like Angular and React are great for building and maintaining complex sites. JavaScript code that manipulates the DOM directly is partial to a new type of security vulnerability, however: DOM-based cross-site scripting attacks, which we'll look at in more detail in Chapter 7.

Note that although JavaScript is the only language a browser typically executes, that doesn't mean you have to write all your client-side code in JavaScript. Many developers use languages like CoffeeScript or TypeScript that are *transpiled* into JavaScript during the build process before being sent to the browser. These languages are subject to the same security vulnerabilities as JavaScript at execution time, so in this book I'll mostly limit our discussions to plain old JavaScript.

Summary

Web servers serve two types of content in response to HTTP requests: static resources, such as images, and dynamic resources, which execute custom code.

Static resources are resources that we can serve directly from a filesystem or a content delivery network to increase the responsiveness of the site. Website owners usually author websites that consist wholly of static resources in a content-management system, which allows nontechnical administrators to edit them directly in the browser.

Dynamic resources, on the other hand, are resources that we often define in the form of templates, HTML that's interspersed with programmatic instructions to be interpreted by the server. They'll typically read data from a database or a cache that informs how the page is rendered. The most common form of database is a SQL database, which stores data in tabular form, with strictly defined rules on the structure of the data. Larger websites often use a NoSQL database, a newer variety of database that relaxes some of the constraints of the traditional SQL database in order to achieve greater scalability. We write dynamic resources in a web programming language, of which there are many.

In the next chapter, you'll look at the process of writing code itself. The key to writing secure, bug-free code is a disciplined development process; I'll show you how you should write, test, build, and deploy your code.

5

HOW PROGRAMMERS WORK

 Building and maintaining a website is an iterative process, not an end goal. Rarely does a web developer build a site and get every feature right the first time. (Unless you're my friend Dave; stop making the rest of us look bad, *Dave.*) In web development, the product evolves and the codebase grows more complex, requiring developers to add features, fix bugs, and restructure code. Redesigns happen as a matter of course.

As a web developer, you need to make and roll out changes to your codebase in an orderly and disciplined fashion. It's common for security vulnerabilities and bugs to creep in over time because of shortcuts taken in the face of deadlines. Most security vulnerabilities are introduced not through a lack of development knowledge, but because of a lack of attention to detail.

This chapter focuses on how you *should* be writing secure code, by adhering to the *Software Development Life Cycle (SDLC)*, a fancy phrase for the process a development team follows when designing new website features, writing code, testing it, and pushing out changes. A chaotic and messy SDLC makes it impossible to track the code you're running and its vulnerabilities, which inevitably leads to a buggy, insecure website. However, a well-structured SDLC allows you to root out bugs and vulnerabilities early in the process to protect your end-product site from attacks.

We'll go through five phases of a good SDLC: design and analysis, writing code, pre-release testing, the release process, and post-release testing and observation. We'll also briefly talk about securing *dependencies*, the third-party software that we use in our websites.

Phase 1: Design and Analysis

The SDLC doesn't begin with writing code; it begins with thinking about what code you *should* be writing. We call this first phase the *design and analysis* phase: you analyze the features you need to add and design their implementation. At the start of a project, this might consist of sketching out brief design aims. But by the time your site is up and running, you need to give changes a little more deliberation, because you don't want to break functionality for existing users.

The most important objective of this phase is identifying the requirements the code is trying to address. Once the development team completes the code, everyone should be able to judge whether the new code changes properly address those requirements. If you're writing code for a client, this phase means meeting with stakeholders and getting them to agree to a list of goals. For in-house development at a company or organization, it mostly means developing and documenting a shared vision of whatever you're building.

Issue-tracking software helps immensely with design and analysis, especially when you're diagnosing and fixing bugs in an existing site. (Issue trackers are also known as *bug trackers* for this reason.) Issue trackers describe individual development goals as *issues*—such as "build a customer checkout page" or "fix the spelling mistake on the home page." Issues are then assigned to individual developers, who can rank their issue by priority, write code to fix them, and mark them as complete. Developers can link specific sets of code changes for the purpose of fixing a bug or adding a feature described in an issue. For large teams, managers can schedule issues with project management software for reporting purposes.

The amount of time you should spend working things out on paper before writing code can vary. Teams that write software for firmware devices or critical systems like nuclear reactors unsurprisingly spend a *lot* of time in the design phase, because they rarely get a chance to fix code after deploying it. Web developers tend to move more quickly.

Phase 2: Writing Code

Once you have completed design and analysis, you can move on to the second phase of the SDLC: writing code. You can write code with a lot of tools, but you should always keep any code that's not a one-off script in *source control software* (also known as *version control*), which allows you to store a backup copy of your codebase, browse previous versions of the codebase, track changes, and annotate the code changes you're making. You can share changes with the rest of your team by pushing code changes to the source *repository*, usually via command line tools or plug-ins to other development tools, before releasing them to the world. *Pushing* your code changes to the centralized repository makes them available to other team members for review. *Releasing* your changes means deploying them to your *production* website—the website that your real users will see.

Using source control also allows you to browse the version of the codebase currently running on the production site, which is key to diagnosing vulnerabilities and investigating and resolving security issues found post-release. When a development team identifies and resolves a security issue, they should look over the code changes that introduced the vulnerability and check whether the changes affected any other parts of the site.

Source control is the number one tool all development teams need to use. (Even a development team of one!) Large companies usually run their own source control servers, while smaller companies and open source developers typically use a third-party hosted service.

Distributed vs. Centralized Version Control

A variety of source control software exists, each with different syntax and features. Of the tools currently available, the most popular is Git, a tool originally created by Linus Torvalds, the founder of Linux, to help organize the development of the Linux kernel. Git is a *distributed version control system*, which means that every copy of the code kept under Git is a fully fledged repository. When a new developer *pulls* (downloads) a local copy of the code from the team repository for the first time, they get not only the latest version of the codebase, but also a complete history of changes to the codebase.

Distributed source control tools track the changes the developer makes, and transmit only those changes when the developer pushes the code. This model of source control differs from older software, which implements a *centralized* server from which developers download and to which they upload whole files.

Git has become popular in no small part because of *GitHub*, a website that makes it straightforward to set up an online Git repository and invite team members. Users can view code stored in GitHub in the browser and can easily document it in the Markdown language. GitHub also includes its own issue tracker and tools to manage competing code changes.

Branching and Merging Code

Source control software allows you to be precise about which code changes get pushed out with each update to your website. Typically, code releases are managed using branches. A *branch* is a logical copy of the codebase, stored either within the source control server or a developer's local repository. Developers can make local changes to their own branch without affecting the *master* codebase, and then *merge* the branch back into the master codebase when they've completed whatever feature or bug fix they were working on.

NOTE   *Larger development teams may have more-elaborate branching schemes. Source control software allows you to create branches off of branches off of branches ad infinitum, since branching is a cheap operation. A large team may have several developers contribute to the same* feature branch *for complex code updates.*

Before a release takes place, several developers might merge different branches into the master codebase. If they've been making different edits to the same files, the source control software automatically attempts to merge those changes. If the differing changes can't be merged automatically, a *merge conflict* occurs, which requires the development team to manually complete the merge process, choosing line by line how competing code changes should be applied. Resolving merge conflicts is the bane of a developer's life: it's extra work that needs doing after you think you've already finished an issue. And usually it's because Dave decided to change the formatting in several thousand Python files. (Thanks, Dave.)

Merge time is an excellent opportunity to do *code reviews*, in which one or more team members look over the code changes and give feedback. A great way to catch potential security vulnerabilities is to follow the *four eyes principle*, which requires two separate people to see every code change before a release. Often, a fresh set of eyes looking over the code can see problems not anticipated by the original author. (Cyclopes are terrible coders, so it's recommended that you double up on their reviews.)

Git-based tools can formalize code reviews by using pull requests. A *pull request* is a developer's request to merge code into the master codebase, which allows tools like GitHub to ensure that another developer approves changes before the merge occurs. (Source control software often makes the approval of pull requests contingent on all tests passing in a continuous integration system, which we'll discuss in the following section.)

Phase 3: Pre-Release Testing

The third stage of the SDLC is testing. You should release code only after you've tested it thoroughly to catch any potential bugs and ensure that it works correctly. A good testing strategy is key to catching software defects, especially security vulnerabilities, before users experience them or hackers can exploit them. Anyone making code changes should manually test the site's functionality before merging or releasing code. This is a basic level of diligence you should expect from all members of your team.

Catching software defects earlier in the development life cycle saves a lot of time and effort, so you should complement your manual testing with unit testing. *Unit tests* are small scripts within the codebase that make basic assertions about how the code operates by executing various parts of the codebase and testing the output. You should run unit tests as part of your build process, and write unit tests for particularly sensitive or frequently changing areas of your code.

Keep unit tests simple, so that they test isolated functions of the code. Overly complex unit tests that test multiple pieces of functionality at once are *brittle*, prone to breaking as code changes are made. A good unit test, for instance, might assert that only authenticated users can view certain areas of the website, or that passwords have to meet a minimum complexity requirement. Good unit tests additionally act as a form of documentation, illustrating how the code should operate if implemented correctly.

Coverage and Continuous Integration

When you run a unit test, it calls functions in your main codebase. When you run all your unit tests, the percentage of your codebase that they execute is called your *coverage*. Although aiming for 100 percent test coverage is laudable, it's often impractical, so be careful in choosing which parts of the codebase you write unit tests for. (Besides, complete test coverage doesn't guarantee correct code; just because every code path is executed doesn't mean all scenarios are covered.) Writing good unit tests is a matter of judgment and should be part of a larger risk-assessment strategy. Here's a good rule of thumb: when you discover a bug, write a unit test asserting the correct behavior, and *then* fix the bug. This prevents the issue from reoccurring.

Once you have sufficient test coverage, you should set up a continuous integration server. A *continuous integration server* connects to your source control repository and, whenever code changes are made, checks out a fresh version of the code and runs the build process while executing your unit tests. If the build process fails—perhaps because the unit tests start failing—your development team receives an alert. Continuous integration ensures that you spot software defects early and address them promptly.

Test Environments

Once you've completed all code changes for a release, you should deploy them to a test environment for final testing. A *test environment* (often called a *staging*, *pre-production*, or *quality assurance environment*) should be a fully operational copy of the website, run on dedicated servers. A test environment is essential for detecting software defects such as security vulnerabilities before a release happens. Large development teams often employ *quality assurance (QA)* staff dedicated to testing software in such environments. If you're integrating different sets of code changes together, this is sometimes called *integration testing*.

A good test environment should resemble the production environment as closely as possible, to ensure that the tests are meaningful. You should run your test environment on the same server and database technologies, differing only in the configuration and the version of the code running on it. (You should still apply common sense. Your test environment shouldn't be able to send email to real users, for instance, so impose deliberate limitations to your test environments as needed.)

This process is analogous to a cast and crew of a theatrical play undertaking a dress rehearsal before performing in front of a live audience for the first time. They put on the play in full costume before a small test audience. This allows them to work out the final kinks in their performance in a low-stakes environment, where every detail resembles the real opening-night performance as closely as possible.

Test environments are a key part of secure releases, but they also pose security risks of their own if not properly managed. Test and production environments need to be properly *segregated* at the network layer, meaning that communication between the two environments is impossible. You can't give attackers the chance to compromise your website by allowing them to hop across the network from an unsecured test environment into your production environment.

Test environments usually have their own database, which requires realistic-looking test data in order to allow thorough testing of the site's functionality. A common approach to generating good test data is copying over data from production systems. If you do this, take special care to *scrub* this kind of data-copy of sensitive information, including names, payment details, and passwords. Numerous high-profile data leaks in recent years have been caused by attackers stumbling across improperly scrubbed data in a test environment.

Phase 4: The Release Process

Writing code for a website isn't much use if you don't ever push it out, so let's talk about the fourth phase of the SDLC: the release process. A *release process* for websites involves taking code from source control, copying it onto a web server, and (typically) restarting the web server process. How you achieve this varies according to where you host your site and what technology you use. Whatever your approach, your release process needs to be reliable, reproducible, and revertible.

A *reliable* release process means that you can guarantee what code, dependencies, resources, and configuration files get deployed during the release. If your release process is unreliable, you may not be running the version of the code you think you're running, which is a serious security risk. To ensure that your website deploys files reliably, release scripts typically use *checksums*—digital "fingerprints" that ensure that the files copied onto the server are identical to those held in source control.

A *reproducible* release process is one that you can rerun with the same results, in different environments, or with different versions of the code. Reproducibility means less room for manual error during a release. If your release process requires an administrator to perfectly perform 24 steps in the correct order, you can expect them to make mistakes. Write scripts and automate your release process as much as possible! A reproducible process is also essential for setting up good test environments.

A *revertible* release process allows you to *roll back* releases. Sometimes unexpected contingencies make you want to "undo" a recent release and revert to a prior version of the code. This process should be as seamless as possible. Partially rolled-back code is a disaster waiting to happen, because you may be leaving an insecure configuration in place, or software dependencies with known vulnerabilities. Whatever release process you choose, you need to be able to reliably revert to a previous version of the codebase with minimal fuss.

Options for Standardized Deployment During Releases

Hosting companies have invented *Platform as a Service (PaaS)* solutions that make releasing code easy and reliable. If "in the cloud" refers to running code on other people's servers, using an "as a service" offering refers to running code on other people's servers, with some helpful automation and an administrative website. (Hosting companies have a track record of inventing horrible marketing acronyms.)

Microsoft Azure, Amazon Web Services Elastic Beanstalk, Google App Engine, and Heroku are all PaaS providers that allow developers to release code with a single command line call. The platform takes care of almost everything else required during the release process: setting up virtualized servers, installing the operating system and virtual machines, running your build process (more on this later), loading dependencies, deploying the code to disk, and restarting the web server process. You can monitor and roll back releases in a web console or from the command line, and the platform performs various safety checks to ensure your code deploys cleanly. Using a PaaS-based release process minimizes downtime for your site, ensures a clean deployment of code, and produces a full audit trail.

PaaS solutions impose limitations. In exchange for this convenience and reliability, they support only certain programming languages and operating systems. They allow a limited amount of server configuration, and they don't support complex network layouts. As a result, it can sometimes be difficult to retrofit legacy applications for deployment on this kind of platform.

Infrastructure as a Service and DevOps

If you're not using PaaS, because your application is too complex, too old, or the cost is too prohibitive, you'll typically deploy your code to individual servers. These might be self-hosted, hosted in a data center, or hosted on virtualized servers in an *Infrastructure as a Service (IaaS)* solution such as Amazon Elastic Compute Cloud (EC2). In such a scenario, you're responsible for authoring your own release process.

Historically, companies have employed dedicated systems administrator staff to design and run the release process. However, the rise of *DevOps* (short for *developer operations*) tools has blurred these responsibilities and allowed developers more control in the way their code gets deployed. DevOps tools (which have a variety of evocative names like Puppet, Chef, and Ansible) make it easy to describe standard deployment scenarios and modularize release scripts, giving development teams the power to design their own deployment strategies. This approach tends to be far more reliable than writing custom release scripts to download and copy files onto servers. DevOps tools make it easy to follow best practices because most deployment scenarios are covered by existing "recipes" or scripts.

Containerization

Another approach to standardizing deployment is using containerization. *Containerization* technologies such as Docker allow you to create configuration scripts known as *images* that describe which operating system, disk layout, and third-party software a server should use, and which web application you should deploy on top of the software stack. You deploy images to a *container* that abstracts various functions of the underlying operating system to allow consistent deployment; everything required specifically for the release is described in the image, and the container is a completely generic component.

You can deploy Docker images to real or virtualized servers in a reproducible manner, making for a reliable release process. Developers testing their code locally can use the same exact Docker image as the production site, resulting in fewer surprises when the code is released for real.

Containerization is a relatively new technology, but it promises to make deployment of complex applications more reliable and standardized. A host of associated technologies (for example, Docker Swarm and Kubernetes) allow complex, multiserver network configurations to be described in machine-readable configuration files. This makes rebuilding whole environments much more straightforward. A team could, for instance, easily start up a whole new test environment with multiple web servers and a database, since these individual services and the way they communicate with each other would be described in a configuration file that the hosting service can understand.

The Build Process

Most codebases have a *build process*, invoked from the command line or development tools, that takes the static code and prepares it for deployment. Languages such as Java and C# compile source code into a deployable binary format during the build process, while languages that use package managers download and validate third-party code, also known as *dependencies*, when they run the build process.

Build processes for websites often preprocess client-side assets ready for deployment. Many developers use languages such as TypeScript and CoffeeScript that they need to compile into JavaScript by the build process. Whether JavaScript is coded by hand or generated, build processes usually *minify*, or obfuscate, JavaScript files in order to generate a compressed, less readable, but functionally equivalent version of each JavaScript file that will load more quickly in the browser.

Styling information for websites is typically held in CSS files, as discussed in Chapter 3. Managing CSS files for large websites can be a chore (because styling information is often duplicated in different places and needs to be updated in sync). Web developers often use *CSS pre-processors* such as Sass and SCSS—languages designed to make stylesheets more manageable, which need to be preprocessed into CSS files at build time.

Each programming language has a preferred build tool that your development team should be proficient with. You should run the build process locally before checking any code into source control, so you can be sure the process works before rerunning it during the release process. Use a continuous integration server, as mentioned previously, to make sure this happens.

Database Migration Scripts

Adding new features to a website often requires new database tables or updates to existing tables. Databases store data that needs to persist between releases, so you can't simply wipe down and install a new database with each release. You need to create and then run database *migration scripts* against the database as part of your release process to update your database structures before deploying your code; and undo the scripts if you roll back the code.

Some technologies (for example, Ruby on Rails) allow you to run migration scripts as part of the build process. If you can't run them as part of the build process, you should keep the scripts under source control, and then run them with temporarily elevated permissions on the database during the release window. In some companies, especially large and complex databases often have dedicated *database administrators (DBAs)* who manage this process and grumpily act as gatekeepers to their beloved datastores.

If staff members are able to change database structures outside a release, that's a security risk. We'll discuss various ways to lock down permissions in Chapter 11.

Phase 5: Post-Release Testing and Observation

Once you've deployed your code, you should perform *post-release testing* to ensure that you've deployed it correctly, and that your assumptions about the way the code would execute in production are correct. Theoretically, this post-release testing (often called *smoke testing*) can be pretty cursory if you have a good test environment and a reliable release process. Nevertheless, it's a good idea to pay attention to your gut instincts and be risk-averse when deciding how much testing to perform at each stage of the SDLC. There's a saying that goes, "Continue testing until fear turns into boredom." It captures the appropriate sentiment.

Penetration Testing

Security professionals and ethical hackers often perform *penetration testing*, which tests for security vulnerabilities by externally probing a website. Penetration testing can be useful for both pre-release and post-release testing. Additionally, the development team can employ sophisticated automated penetration testing tools that test websites for common security vulnerabilities by analyzing various URLs and attempting to craft malicious HTTP requests. Penetration testing can be expensive and time-consuming, but it's much, *much* cheaper than getting hacked, so strongly consider adding it your testing procedures.

Monitoring, Logging, and Error Reporting

Once you've released your code, your production environment needs to be observable at runtime. This helps administrators spot unusual and potentially malicious behavior and diagnose issues as they occur. Post-release observation should happen in the form of three activities: logging, monitoring, and error reporting.

Logging, the practice of having code write to a log file as the software application performs actions, helps administrators see what a web server is doing at any given time. Your code should log every HTTP request (with a timestamp, URL, and the HTTP response code), as well as significant actions performed by users (for example, authentication and password-reset requests) and the site itself (for example, sending email and calling APIs).

You should make logs available to administrators at runtime (either on the command line or through a web console) and archive them for later reading (in case postmortems are needed). Adding log statements to your code helps diagnose problems that occur on your site, but be careful not to write sensitive details like passwords and credit card information on your logs in case an attacker ever manages to get access to them.

Monitoring is the practice of measuring response times and other metrics on your website at runtime. Monitoring your web server and database helps administrators spot high-load scenarios or degraded performance by firing alerts when network speeds slow or database queries take a long time. You should pass HTTP and database response times into monitoring software, which should, in turn, raise alerts when server and database response times pass certain thresholds. Many cloud platforms have monitoring software built in, so take the time to configure your error conditions and your chosen alerting system appropriately.

You should use *error reporting* to capture and record unexpected errors in the code. You can establish error conditions by either picking them out of logs or capturing and recording them in the code itself. You can then collate those error conditions in a datastore you make available to administrators. Many security intrusions exploit badly handled error conditions, so be sure to pay attention to unexpected errors as they occur.

Third-party services such as Rollbar and Airbrake supply plug-ins that allow you to collect errors with a few lines of code, so if you don't have the time or inclination to set up your own error-reporting system, consider using these types of services. Alternatively, log-scraping tools such as Splunk allow you to pick out errors from log files and make sense of them.

Dependency Management

One thing you need to consider alongside the regular SDLC is dependency management. A curious fact about modern web development is that you'll likely write only a small minority of the code that runs your website. Your site will typically depend on operating system code, a programming language runtime and associated libraries, possibly a virtual machine, and a web server process running third-party code libraries. All of these third-party tools that you'll have to rely on to support your website's code are known as *dependencies*. (In other words, the software that *your* software depends on to run.)

Experts in their field write each of these dependencies, saving you the burden of having to write your own memory management or low-level TCP semantics. These experts also have a strong incentive to stay on top of security vulnerabilities and issue patches as they arise, so you should take advantage of the resources they provide!

Using other people's code requires diligence on your part. A secure SDLC should include a process for reviewing third-party libraries and determining when patches need to be applied. This often needs to happen outside the regular development cycle, since hackers won't wait until your next scheduled release date to begin trying to exploit a security vulnerability. Staying ahead of security advisories and deploying patches for other people's code is just as key as securing the code your team writes. We'll look at how to do this in Chapter 14.

Summary

In this chapter, you learned that a well-structured software development life cycle allows you to avoid bugs and software vulnerabilities.

- You should document design goals by using issue-tracking software.
- You should keep code in source control to make older versions of the code available for inspection, and to make it easy to organize code reviews.
- Before a release, you should test code in a dedicated and isolated test environment that resembles your production environment and that treats your data with utmost care.
- You should have a reliable, reproducible, and revertible release process. If you have a scripted build process that generates assets ready for deployment, you should run it regularly and with unit tests in a continuous integration environment to highlight potential problems early in the development life cycle.

- After a release, you should use penetration testing to detect website vulnerabilities before a hacker can make use of them. You should also use monitoring, logging, and error reporting to detect and diagnose problems with your running site.
- You should stay ahead of security advisories for any third-party code you use, because you may need to deploy patches outside your regular release cycle.

In the next chapter, you'll (finally!) begin to look at specific software vulnerabilities and how to protect against them. You'll begin by looking at one of the biggest threats websites face: malicious input designed to inject code into your web server.

PART II

THE THREATS

6

INJECTION ATTACKS

Now that you have a solid grasp of how the internet works, let's focus on specific vulnerabilities and the methods hackers use to exploit them. This chapter covers *injection attacks*, which occur when the attacker injects external code into an application in an effort to take control of the application or read sensitive data.

Recall that the internet is an example of a *client-server architecture*, meaning that a web server handles connections from many clients at once. Most clients are web browsers, responsible for generating HTTP requests to the web server as a user navigates the website. The web server returns HTTP responses containing the HTML that makes up the content of the website's pages.

Because the web server controls the website's content, server-side code naturally expects specific types of user interactions to occur, and therefore expects the browser to generate specific types of HTTP requests. For instance, the server expects to see a GET request to a new URL each time the user clicks a link, or a POST request if they enter their login credentials and click Submit.

However, it's perfectly possible for a browser to generate unexpected HTTP requests to a server. In addition, web servers happily accept HTTP requests from any type of client, not just browsers. A programmer equipped with an HTTP client library can write scripts that send requests to arbitrary URLs on the internet. The hacking tools we reviewed in Chapter 1 do exactly that.

Server-side code has no reliable way of telling whether a script or a browser generated an HTTP request, because the contents of the HTTP request are indistinguishable regardless of the client. The best a server can do is to check the User-Agent header, which is *supposed* to describe the type of *agent* that generated the request, but scripts and hacking tools typically *spoof* the contents of this header, so it matches what a browser would send.

Knowing all of this, hackers attacking a website frequently pass malicious code in an HTTP request so that it tricks the server into executing the code. This is the basis of an injection attack on a website.

Injection attacks are astonishingly common on the internet and, if successful, can be devastating in their impact. As a web developer, you'll need to know all the ways they can occur and how to defend against them. When writing website code, it's important to consider what *could* come through in the HTTP requests being handled by the site, not just what you expect to come through. In this chapter, you'll look at four types of injection attacks: SQL injection attacks, command injection attacks, remote code execution attacks, and attacks that exploit file upload vulnerabilities.

SQL Injection

SQL injection attacks target websites that use an underlying SQL database and construct data queries to the database in an insecure fashion. SQL injection attacks pose one of the greatest risks to websites because SQL databases are so common. This was evident in 2008, when hackers stole 130 million credit card numbers from Heartland Payment Systems, a payment processor that stores credit card details and handles payments for merchants. The hackers used a SQL injection attack to access the web servers that handled payment data, which was a disaster for a company that relies on the assurance of their information's security to do business.

Let's begin by reviewing how SQL databases work, so that we can get to the heart of how SQL injection works and how we can stop it.

What Is SQL?

Structured Query Language, or *SQL*, extracts data and data structures in relational databases. Relational databases store data in tables; each row in a table is a data item (for example, a user, or a product being sold). SQL syntax allows applications such as web servers to add rows to the database by using INSERT statements, read rows by using SELECT statements, update rows by using UPDATE statements, and remove rows by using DELETE statements.

Consider the SQL statements that a web server might run behind the scenes when you sign up on a website, as shown in Listing 6-1.

```
❶ INSERT INTO users (email, encrypted_password)
   VALUES ('billy@gmail.com', '$10$WMT9Y')
❷ SELECT * FROM users WHERE email = 'billy@gmail.com'
   AND encrypted_password = '$10$WMT9Y'
❸ UPDATE USERS users encrypted_password ='3D$MW$10Z'
   WHERE email='billy@gmail.com'
❹ DELETE FROM users WHERE email = 'billy@gmail.com'
```

Listing 6-1: Typical SQL statements that a web server might run when a user interacts with a website

SQL databases typically store information about the website's users in a users table. When a user first signs up and chooses a username and password, the web server runs an INSERT statement on the database to create a new row in the users table ❶. The next time a user logs in to the website, the web server runs a SELECT statement to attempt to find the corresponding row in the users table ❷. If the user changes their password, the web server runs an UPDATE statement to update the corresponding row in the users table ❸. Finally, if the user closes their account, the website might run a DELETE statement to remove their row from the users table ❹.

For each interaction, the web server is responsible for taking parts of the HTTP request (for example, the username and password entered into a login form) and constructing a SQL statement to run against the database. The actual execution of the statement happens through the *database driver*, a dedicated code library used to communicate with the database.

Anatomy of a SQL Injection Attack

SQL injection attacks occur when the web server insecurely constructs the SQL statement it passes to the database driver. This allows the attacker to pass arguments via the HTTP request that cause the driver to perform actions other than those the developer intends.

Let's look at an insecurely constructed SQL statement that reads user data from the database when a user attempts to log in to a website, as shown in the Java code in Listing 6-2.

```
Connection connection = DriverManager.getConnection(DB_URL, DB_USER, DB_PASSWORD);
Statement statement = connection.createStatement();
String sql = "SELECT * FROM users WHERE email='" + email +
        "' AND encrypted_password='" + password + "'";
statement.executeQuery(sql);
```

Listing 6-2: An insecure method of reading user data from the database during a login attempt

The construction of this SQL statement isn't secure! This snippet uses the email and password parameters taken from the HTTP request, and inserts them directly into the SQL statement. Because the parameters aren't checked for SQL control characters (such as ') that change the meaning of the SQL statement, a hacker can craft input that bypasses the website's authentication system.

An example of this is shown in Listing 6-3. In this example, the attacker passes the user email parameter as billy@gmail.com'--, which terminates the SQL statement early and causes the password-checking logic to not execute:

```
statement.executeQuery(
    "SELECT * FROM users WHERE email='billy@gmail.com'❶--' AND encrypted_password='Z$DSA92HO'❷");
```

Listing 6-3: Using SQL injection to bypass authentication

The database driver executes only the SQL statement ❶, and ignores everything that comes after it ❷. In this type of SQL injection attack, the single quote character (') closes the email argument early, and the SQL comment syntax (--) tricks the database driver into ignoring the end of the statement that does password checking. This SQL statement allows the attacker to log in as *any* user without having to know their password! All the attacker has to do is add the ' and -- characters to the user's email address in the login form.

This is a relatively simple example of a SQL injection attack. A more advanced attack might cause the database driver to run additional commands on the database. Listing 6-4 shows a SQL injection attack that runs a DROP command to remove the users table entirely, in order to corrupt the database.

```
statement.executeQuery("SELECT * FROM users WHERE email='billy@gmail.com';❶
DROP TABLE users;❷--' AND encrypted_password='Z$DSA92HO'");
```

Listing 6-4: A SQL injection attack in progress

In this scenario, the attacker passes the email parameter as billy@gmail .com'; DROP TABLE users;--. The semicolon character (;) terminates the first SQL statement ❶, after which the attacker inserts an additional, destructive statement ❷. The database driver will run both statements, leaving your database in a corrupt state!

If your website is vulnerable to SQL injection, an attacker can often run arbitrary SQL statements against your database, allowing them to bypass authentication; read, download, and delete data at will; or even inject malicious JavaScript into the pages rendered to your users. To scan websites for SQL injection vulnerabilities, hacking tools like Metasploit can be used to crawl websites and test HTTP parameters with potential exploits. If your site is vulnerable to SQL injection attacks, you can be sure that somebody will eventually take advantage of it.

Mitigation 1: Use Parameterized Statements

To protect against SQL injection attacks, your code needs to construct SQL strings using bind parameters. *Bind parameters* are placeholder characters that the database driver will safely replace with some supplied inputs—like the email or password values shown in Listing 6-1. A SQL statement containing bind parameters is called a *parameterized statement.*

SQL injection attacks use "control characters" that have special meaning in SQL statements to "jump out" of the context and change the whole semantics of the SQL statement. When you use bind parameters, these control characters are prefixed with "escape characters" that tell the database not to treat the following character as a control character. This escaping of control characters defuses potential injection attacks.

A securely constructed SQL statement using bind parameters should look like Listing 6-5.

```
Connection connection = DriverManager.getConnection(DB_URL, DB_USER, DB_PASSWORD);
Statement statement = connection.createStatement();
❶ String sql = "SELECT * FROM users WHERE email = ? and encrypted_password = ?";
❷ statement.executeQuery(sql, email, password);
```

Listing 6-5: Using bind parameters to protect against SQL injection

This code constructs the SQL query in parameterized form using ? as the bind parameter ❶. The code then *binds* the input values for each parameter to the statement ❷, asking the database driver to insert the parameter values into the SQL statement while securely handling any control characters. If an attacker attempts to hack this code using the method outlined in Listing 6-4 by passing in a username of billy@email.com'--, your securely constructed SQL statement will defuse the attack, as shown in Listing 6-6.

```
statement.executeQuery(
  "SELECT * FROM users WHERE email = ? AND encrypted_password = ?",
  "billy@email.com'--,",
  "Z$DSA92HO");
```

Listing 6-6: The SQL injection attack is defused.

Because the database driver makes sure not to terminate the SQL statement early, this SELECT statement will safely return *no* users, and the attack should fail. Parameterized statements ensure that the database driver treats all control characters (such as ', --, and ;) as an *input* to the SQL statement, rather than as part of the SQL statement. If you're not sure whether your website is using parameterized statements, go check immediately! SQL injection is probably the biggest risk your website will face.

Similar types of injection attacks may be possible whenever a web server communicates with a separate backend by constructing a statement in the backend's native language. This includes NoSQL databases like MongoDB and Apache Cassandra, distributed caches like Redis and Memcached, and directories that implement the Lightweight Directory Access Protocol (LDAP). Libraries that communicate with these platforms have their own implementation of bind parameters, so be sure to understand how they work and to use them in your code.

Mitigation 2: Use Object-Relational Mapping

Many web server libraries and frameworks abstract away the explicit construction of SQL statements in code and allow you to access data objects by using object-relational mapping. *Object-relational mapping (ORM)* libraries map rows in database tables to code objects in memory, meaning the developer generally doesn't have to write their own SQL statements in order to read from and update the database. This architecture protects against SQL injection attacks under most circumstances, but can still be vulnerable if custom SQL statements are used—so it's important to understand how your ORM works behind the scenes.

The ORM that people are probably most familiar with is the Ruby on Rails ActiveRecord framework. Listing 6-7 shows a simple line of Rails code that finds a user in a secure fashion.

```
User.find_by(email: "billy@gmail.com")
```

Listing 6-7: Ruby on Rails code that looks up a user by email in a way that is protected against injection attacks

Because ORMs use bind parameters under the hood, they protect against injection attacks in most cases. However, most ORMs also have backdoors that allow the developer to write raw SQL if needed. If you use these types of functions, you need to be careful about how you construct the SQL statements. For instance, Listing 6-8 shows Rails code that *is* vulnerable to injection.

```
def find_user(email, password)
  User.where("email = '" + email + "' and encrypted_password = '" + password + "'")
end
```

Listing 6-8: Ruby on Rails code that is vulnerable to injection

Because this code passes part of the SQL statements as a raw string, an attacker can pass in special characters to manipulate the SQL statement that Rails generates. If the attacker can set the password variable to ' OR 1=1, they can run a SQL statement that disables the password check, as shown in Listing 6-9.

```
SELECT * FROM users WHERE email='billy@gmail.com' AND encrypted_password ='' OR 1=1
```

Listing 6-9: The 1=1 statement, which is trivially true, disables the password check.

The final clause of this SQL statement disables the password check, allowing the attacker to log in as that user. You can securely call the where function in Rails by using bind parameters, as shown in Listing 6-10.

```
def find_user(email, encrypted_password)
  User.where(["email = ? and encrypted_password = ?", email, encrypted_password])
end
```

Listing 6-10: Secure use of the where function

In this scenario, the ActiveRecord framework will securely handle any SQL control characters an attacker adds to the `email` or `password` parameter.

Bonus Mitigation: Use Defense in Depth

As a rule of thumb, you should always secure your website with redundancies. It's not enough to check your code line by line for vulnerabilities. You need to consider and enforce security at every level of the stack, allowing failures at one level to be mitigated by other strategies. This is an approach called *defense in depth*.

Consider how you secure your home. The most important defense is installing locks on all doors and windows, but it also helps to have a burglar alarm, security cameras, household insurance, and maybe a large bad-tempered dog, in order to cover all eventualities.

When it comes to preventing SQL injection, defense in depth means using bind parameters, but also taking additional steps to minimize the harm in case an attacker *still* finds a way to successfully execute injection attacks. Let's look at a couple of other ways to mitigate the risk of injection attacks.

Principle of Least Privilege

An additional way to mitigate injection attacks is to follow the *principle of least privilege*, which demands that every process and application run only with the permissions it needs to perform its permitted functions, and no more. This means that if an attacker injects code into your web server and compromises a particular software component, the damage they can do is limited to the actions permissible by that particular software component.

If your web server talks to a database, make sure the account it uses to log into the database has limited permissions on the data. Most websites need to run only SQL statements that fall under the subset of SQL called the *data manipulation language (DML)*, which includes the SELECT, INSERT, UPDATE, and DELETE statements we discussed earlier.

A subset of the SQL language called *data definition language (DDL)* uses CREATE, DROP, and MODIFY statements to create, drop, and modify the table structures in the database itself. Web servers generally don't require permissions to execute DDL statements, so don't grant them the DDL set of permissions at runtime! Narrowing the web server privileges to the minimal DML set reduces the harm an attacker can do if they discover a code vulnerability.

Blind and Nonblind SQL Injection

Hackers distinguish between blind and nonblind SQL injection attacks. If your website's error message leaks sensitive information to the client, like the message Unique constraint violated: this email address already exists in users table, this is a *nonblind* SQL attack. In this scenario, the attacker gets immediate feedback on their attempts to compromise your system.

If you keep your error messages to the client more generic, like the messages `Could not find this username and password` or `An unexpected error occurred`, this is a *blind* SQL attack. This scenario means the attacker is effectively operating in the dark and has less to work with. Websites vulnerable to nonblind injection attacks are much easier to compromise, so avoid leaking information in error messages.

Command Injection

Another type of injection attack is *command injection*, which attackers can use to exploit a website that makes insecure command line calls to the underlying operating system. If your web application makes command line calls, make sure to construct your command strings securely. Otherwise, attackers can craft HTTP requests that execute arbitrary operating system commands, and seize control of your application.

For many programming languages, constructing command strings to invoke operating systems is actually pretty unusual. Java, for example, runs in a virtual machine, so although you *could* call out to the operating system by using the `java.lang.Runtime` class, Java applications are generally designed to be portable between different operating systems, so relying on the availability of specific operating systems functions would go against its philosophy.

Command line calls are more common for interpreted languages. PHP is designed to follow the Unix philosophy—programs should do one thing and communicate with each other via text streams—so it's common for PHP applications to call other programs via the command line. Similarly, Python and Ruby are popular for scripting tasks, so they make it easy to execute commands at the operating system level.

Anatomy of a Command Injection Attack

If your website makes use of command line calls, make sure an attacker can't trick the web server into injecting extra commands into the execution call. Imagine, for instance, that you have a simple website that does `nslookup` to resolve domains and IP addresses. The PHP code takes the domain or IP address from the HTTP request and constructs an operating system call as shown in Listing 6-11.

```php
<?php
    if (isset($_GET['domain'])) {
        echo '<pre>';
        $domain = $_GET['domain']❶;
        $lookup = system("nslookup {$domain❷}");
        echo($lookup);
        echo '</pre>';
    }
?>
```

Listing 6-11: PHP code receiving an HTTP request and constructing an operating system call

The domain parameter is extracted from the HTTP request at ❶. Because the code does not escape the domain argument when constructing the command string ❷, an attacker can craft a malicious URL and tag an extra command on the end, as shown in Figure 6-1.

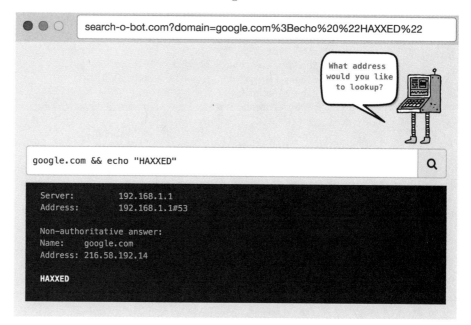

Figure 6-1: Using the URL to inject a malicious command

Here the attacker sends a domain parameter with the value google.com && echo "HAXXED", and the browser URL-encodes the whitespace and non-alphanumeric characters. The && syntax in Unix concatenates separate commands. Because our PHP code doesn't strip such control characters, the attacker carefully constructs the HTTP request to append an extra command. Two separate commands will get executed in this scenario: the expected nslookup command that looks up *google.com*, followed by the *injected* command echo "HAXXED".

In this case, the injected command is a harmless echo command, which simply prints out "HAXXED" in the HTTP response. However, an attacker can use this vulnerability to inject and execute any command they choose on your server. With a bit of effort, they can explore the filesystem, read sensitive information, and compromise the entire application. Command line access on a web server gives the attacker complete freedom to take control of the system unless you take deliberate steps to lessen the impact.

Mitigation: Escape Control Characters

As with SQL injection, you can defend against command injection by properly escaping inputs from the HTTP request. This means replacing sensitive control characters (like the & character in our example) with a safe alternative. How you do this depends on the operating system and programing language you're using. To make the PHP code in Listing 6-11 more secure, we simply need to use a call to escapeshellarg, as shown in Listing 6-12.

```php
<?php
    if (isset($_GET['domain'])) {
        echo '<pre>';
        $domain = escapeshellarg❶($_GET['domain']);
        $lookup = system("nslookup {$domain}");
        echo($lookup);
        echo '</pre>';
    }
?>
```

Listing 6-12: PHP code escaping inputs from the HTTP request

The call to escapeshellarg ❶ ensures that attackers can't inject extra commands via the domain parameter.

Python and Ruby can prevent potential command injection attacks too.

In Python, the call() function should be invoked with an array, rather than a string, to prevent attackers from tagging extra commands onto the end, as shown in Listing 6-13.

```python
from subprocess import call
call(["nslookup", domain])
```

Listing 6-13: The call function in Python's subprocess module

In Ruby, the system() function makes a command line call. Supply it with an array of arguments, rather than a string, to ensure that attackers can't sneak in extra commands, as shown in Listing 6-14.

```ruby
system("nslookup", domain)
```

Listing 6-14: The system() function in Ruby

As with SQL injection, following the principle of least privilege also helps limit the impact of successful command injection attacks. Your web server process should run with only the permissions it requires. For instance, you should limit the directories the web server process can read from and write to. On Linux, you can use the chroot command to prevent the process from exploring outside a designated root directory. You should try to limit the network access your web server has, too, by configuring firewalls and access control lists on the network. These steps will make it much harder for a hacker to exploit a command injection vulnerability, because even if they can execute commands, they can't do anything besides read files in the web server's running directory.

Remote Code Execution

So far, you've seen how vulnerabilities can creep in when web code constructs a call to databases, as with SQL injection, or to the operating system it's running on, as with command injection. In other circumstances, attackers can inject malicious code to be executed in the language of the web server itself, a tactic called *remote code execution*. Remote code execution attacks on websites are rarer than the injection attacks we discussed earlier, but every bit as dangerous.

Anatomy of a Remote Code Execution Attack

An attacker can achieve remote code execution by discovering a vulnerability in a particular type of web server, and then creating *exploit scripts* to target websites running on that web server technology. The exploit script incorporates malicious code in the body of the HTTP request, encoded in such a way that the server will read and execute that code when the request is handled. The techniques used to perform remote execution attacks vary significantly. Security researchers will analyze codebases for common web servers, looking for vulnerabilities that permit malicious code to be injected.

In early 2013, researchers discovered a vulnerability in Ruby on Rails that permitted attackers to inject their own Ruby code into the server process. Because the Rails framework automatically parses requests according to their Content-Type header, security researchers noticed that if they created an XML request with an embedded YAML object (a markup language commonly used in the Rails community for storing configuration data), they could trick the parsing process into executing arbitrary code.

Mitigation: Disable Code Execution During Deserialization

Remote code execution vulnerabilities usually occur when web server software uses insecure serialization. *Serialization* is the process of converting an in-memory data structure into a stream of binary data, usually for the purpose of passing the data structure across a network. *Deserialization* refers to the reverse process that occurs at the other end, when the binary data is converted back into a data structure.

Serialization libraries exist in every major programming language and are widely used. Some serialization libraries, such as the YAML parser used by Rails, allow data structures to execute code as they reinitialize themselves in memory. This is a useful feature if you trust the source of the serialized data, but can be *very* dangerous if you don't, because it can permit arbitrary code execution.

If a web server uses deserialization to handle data coming in from HTTP requests, it needs to defuse any serialization libraries it uses by disabling any code-execution capabilities; otherwise, an attacker may be able to find a way to inject code directly into the web server process. We can typically disable code execution via a relevant configuration setting that will allow your web server software to deserialize data without executing code.

As a developer who uses a web server to build sites, rather than one who writes the web server code itself, protecting against remote code execution in your web stack usually amounts to staying aware of security advisories. You're unlikely to be writing your own serialization libraries, so be aware of where your codebase uses third-party serialization libraries. Make sure to turn off active code execution features in your own code, and keep an eye out for vulnerability announcements issued by your web server vendor.

File Upload Vulnerabilities

The final type of injection attack we'll look at in this chapter takes advantage of vulnerabilities in file upload functions. Websites use *file upload functions* for a variety of purposes: letting users add images to their profile or posts, adding attachments to messages, submitting paperwork, sharing documents with other users, and so on. Browsers make it easy to upload files via built-in file-upload widgets and JavaScript APIs that allow you to drag files onto a web page and send them asynchronously to the server.

However, browsers aren't exactly careful about checking the contents of a file. Attackers can easily abuse file upload functions by injecting malicious code into an uploaded file. Web servers typically treat uploaded files like large blobs of binary data, so it's pretty easy for an attacker to upload a malicious payload without the web server detecting it. Even if your site has JavaScript code that checks a file's content before uploading it, an attacker can write scripts to post file data to the server-side endpoint directly, circumventing any security measures you put in place on the client side.

Let's see how attackers typically exploit file upload functions so that we identify the various security weaknesses that we need to plug.

Anatomy of a File Upload Attack

As an example of a file upload vulnerability, let's look at how an attacker could potentially abuse the profile image upload function of your site. The attacker first writes a small *web shell*, a simple executable script that will take an argument from an HTTP request, execute it on the command line, and output the result. Web shells are a common tool used by hackers attempting to compromise a web server. Listing 6-15 shows an example of a web shell written in PHP.

```php
<?php
  if(isset($_REQUEST['cmd'])) {
    $cmd = ($_REQUEST['cmd']);
    system($cmd);
  } else {
    echo "What is your bidding?";
  }
?>
```

Listing 6-15: A web shell written in the PHP language

The attacker saves this script as *hack.php* on their computer and uploads it as their profile "image" on your site. PHP files are typically treated by operating systems as *executable* files, which is key to making this attack work. Clearly a file ending with *.php* isn't a valid image file, but the attacker can fairly easily disable any JavaScript file-type checking done during the upload process.

Once the attacker has uploaded their "image" file, their website profile page will show a missing image icon, because their profile image is corrupted and not actually an image. However, at this point they have achieved their real aim: smuggling the web shell file onto your server, which means their malicious code is now deployed to your site, waiting to be executed in some fashion.

Because the web shell is available on a public URL, the attacker has potentially created a backdoor for executing the malicious code. If your server's operating system has a PHP runtime installed, and the file was written to disk with executable privileges during the upload process, the attacker can pass commands to run the web shell simply by invoking the URL that corresponds to their profile image.

To perform a command injection attack, the hacker can pass a `cmd` argument to the web shell to execute arbitrary operating system commands on your server, as shown in Figure 6-2.

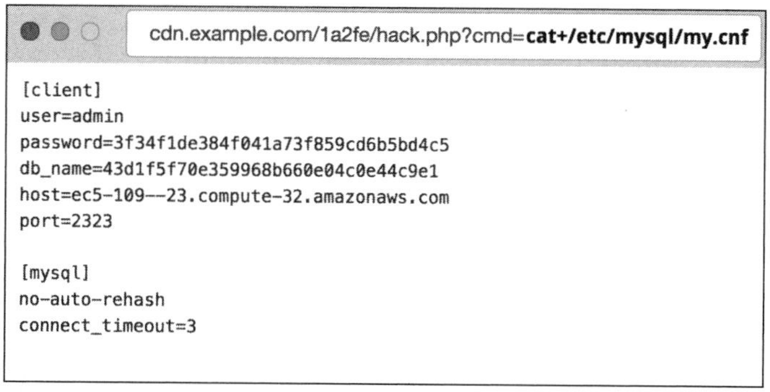

```
● ● ○        cdn.example.com/1a2fe/hack.php?cmd=cat+/etc/mysql/my.cnf

[client]
user=admin
password=3f34f1de384f041a73f859cd6b5bd4c5
db_name=43d1f5f70e359968b660e04c0e44c9e1
host=ec5-109--23.compute-32.amazonaws.com
port=2323

[mysql]
no-auto-rehash
connect_timeout=3
```

Figure 6-2: If your file upload function is vulnerable, a hacker could use a web shell to access your database credentials.

In this scenario, the attacker can explore your filesystem. The attacker has taken advantage of your file upload function to gain the same access to your operating system as they would with a command injection attack.

Mitigations

You can use several mitigations to protect yourself against vulnerabilities in file upload code. The most important mitigations ensure that any uploaded files can't be executed as code. Following the principle of defense in depth, you should also analyze uploaded files and reject any that appear to be corrupt or malicious.

Mitigation 1: Host Files on a Secure System

The first, most important approach to securing file upload functions is to ensure that your web server treats uploaded files as inert rather than executable objects. You can do this by hosting your uploaded files in a content delivery network (CDN) such as Cloudflare or Akamai, as described in Chapter 4, which offloads the security burden to a third party who stores your files securely.

CDNs have other nonsecurity-related benefits too. CDNs serve files extremely fast to the browser, and can put them through processing pipelines as you upload them. Many CDNs offer sophisticated JavaScript upload widgets that you can add with a few lines of code, and that provide bonus features like image cropping.

If for some reason a CDN isn't an option, you can get many of the same benefits by storing uploaded files in cloud-based storage (for example, Amazon Simple Storage Service, or S3) or a dedicated content management system. Both approaches provide secure storage that defuses all web shells as they're uploaded. (Although, if you're hosting your own content management system, you'll have to make sure to configure it correctly.)

Mitigation 2: Ensure Uploaded Files Cannot Be Executed

If using a CDN or content management system isn't an option, you need to take the same steps to secure your files that a CDN or content management does behind the scenes. This means ensuring that all files are written to disk without executable permissions, separating uploaded files into a particular directory or partition (so they aren't intermingled with code), and *hardening* your servers so that only the minimally required software is installed. (Uninstall the PHP engine if you aren't using it!) It's a good idea to rename files as you upload them too, so you don't write files with dangerous file extensions to disk.

The ways to achieve these ends vary depending on your hosting technology, operating system, and the programming language you use. If you're running a Python web server on Linux, for instance, you can set file permissions when creating a file by using the os module, as shown in Listing 6-16.

```
import os
file_descriptor = os.open("/path/to/file", os.O_WRONLY | os.O_CREAT, 0o600)
with os.fdopen(open(file_descriptor, "wb")) as file_handle:
  file_handle.write(...)
```

Listing 6-16: Writing a file with read-write (but not execute) permissions in Python on Linux

Removing unneeded software from your operating system is always a good idea, because it gives a hacker fewer tools to play with. The Center for Internet Security (CIS) provides prehardened operating system images that make a good starting point. They're available as Docker images or as Amazon Machine Images (AMIs) in the Amazon Web Services Marketplace.

Mitigation 3: Validate the Content of Uploaded Files

If you're uploading files with a known file type, consider adding some file-type checking in your code. Make sure the Content-Type header in the HTTP request of the upload matches the expected file type, but be aware that an attacker can easily spoof the header.

It's possible to validate the file type after the file has been uploaded, particularly with image files, so it's a good idea to implement this feature in your server-side code, as shown in Listing 6-17. Your mileage should vary, though; clever hackers in the past have infiltrated various systems by designing payloads that are valid for more than one type of file format.

```
>>> import imghdr
>>> imghdr.what('/tmp/what_is_this.dat')
'gif'
```

Listing 6-17: Reading the file headers to validate a file format in Python

Mitigation 4: Run Antivirus Software

Finally, if you're running on a server platform that's prone to viruses (hello, Microsoft Windows!) make sure you're running up-to-date antivirus software. File upload functions are an open door to virus payloads.

Summary

In this chapter, you learned about various injection attacks, whereby an attacker crafts malicious HTTP requests to take control of backend systems.

SQL injection attacks take advantage of web code that doesn't securely construct SQL strings when communicating with a SQL database. You can mitigate SQL injection by using bind parameters when communicating with the database driver.

Command injection attacks take advantage of code that makes insecure calls to operating system functions. You can similarly defuse command injection through correct use of binding.

Remote code execution vulnerabilities allow hackers to run exploits inside the web server process itself, and typically stem from insecure serialization libraries. Make sure to stay on top of any security advisories for the serialization libraries you use, and for your web server software.

File upload functions often enable command injection attacks if your file upload functionality writes uploaded files to disk with executable privileges. Make sure to write uploads to a third-party system or to disk with appropriate permissions, and do whatever you can to validate the file type as you upload them.

You can mitigate the risks around all types of injection attacks by following the principle of least privilege: processes and software components should run with only the permissions they require to perform their assigned tasks, and no more. This approach reduces the harm an attack can do if they inject harmful code. Examples of following the principle of least privilege include limiting file and network access for your web server process, and connecting to your database under an account with limited permissions.

In the next chapter, you'll look at how hackers can use JavaScript vulnerabilities to attack your website.

7

CROSS-SITE SCRIPTING ATTACKS

In the previous chapter, you saw how attackers can inject code into web servers to compromise websites. If your web server is secure, a hacker's next best injection target is the web browser. Browsers obediently execute any JavaScript code that appears in a web page, so if an attacker can find a way to inject malicious JavaScript into a user's browser while the user views your website, that user is in for a bad time. We call this type of code injection a *cross-site scripting (XSS) attack*.

JavaScript can read or modify any part of a web page, so there's a lot an attacker can do with cross-site scripting vulnerabilities. They can steal login credentials or other sensitive information like credit card numbers as the user types them in. If JavaScript can read the HTTP session information, they can hijack a user's session entirely, allowing them to log in as that user remotely. (You'll learn more about session hijacking in Chapter 10).

Cross-site scripting is a remarkably common type of attack, and the dangers it poses are clear. This chapter presents the three most common types of cross-site scripting attacks and explains how to protect against them.

Stored Cross-Site Scripting Attacks

Websites routinely generate and render HTML using information stored in a database. Retail websites will store product information in a database, and social media sites will store user conversations. Websites will take content from the database according to the URL the user has navigated to, and interpolate it into the page to produce the finished HTML.

Any page content coming from the database is a potential attack vector for hackers. Attackers will attempt to inject JavaScript code into the database so that the web server will write out the JavaScript when it renders HTML. We call this type of attack a *stored cross-site scripting* attack: the JavaScript is written to the database, but executed in the browser when an unsuspecting victim views a particular page on the site.

Malicious JavaScript can be planted in a database by using the SQL injection method described in Chapter 6, but attackers will more commonly insert malicious code through legitimate avenues. For instance, if a website allows users to post comments, the site will store the comment text in a database and display it back to other users who view the same comment thread. In this scenario, an easy way for a hacker to perform a cross-site scripting attack is to write a comment containing a <script> tag to the database. If the website fails to construct HTML securely, the <script> tag will get written out whenever the page is rendered to other users, and the JavaScript will be executed in the victim's browser.

Let's look at a concrete example. Imagine you run a popular website for people who like to bake, *https://breddit.com*. Your site encourages users to participate in discussion threads about bread-related topics. While using the online forum for discussion, the users themselves contribute most of the site's content. When a user adds a post, your website records it to the database and shows it to other users participating in the same thread. This is a perfect opportunity for an attacker to inject some JavaScript through a comment, as shown in Figure 7-1.

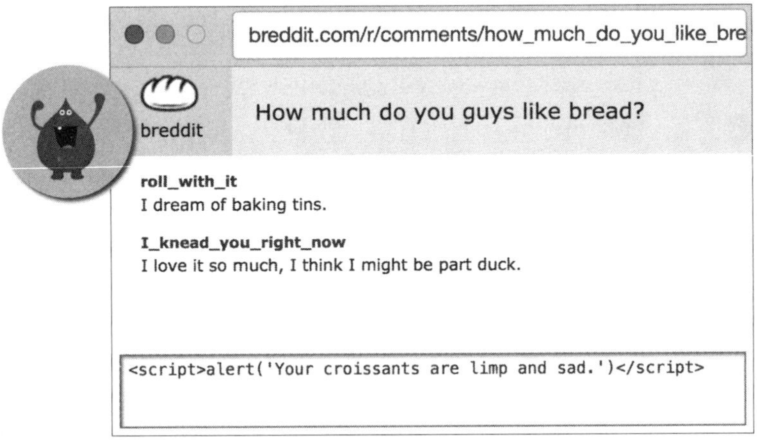

Figure 7-1: An attacker injects JavaScript through a comment.

If your website doesn't escape the injected script when it renders the HTML (as we'll discuss in the following section), the next user to view the thread will have the attacker's `<script>` tag written out to their browser and executed, as shown in Figure 7-2.

Figure 7-2: An attacker's `<script>` tag is written out to the victim's browser and executed.

A rogue `alert()` dialog is more of an annoyance than a genuine threat, but attackers typically start with this approach to check whether cross-site scripting attacks are possible. If an attacker can call the `alert()` function, they can escalate to more dangerous attacks, like stealing other users' sessions, or redirecting victims to harmful sites. The baking community would never feel safe online again!

Comment threads aren't the only place that can exhibit this type of vulnerability. *Any* user-controlled content is a potential avenue of attack that you need to secure. Attackers have performed cross-site scripting attacks by injecting malicious script tags into usernames, profile pages, and online reviews, for example. Let's look at a couple of straightforward protections you should implement.

Mitigation 1: Escape HTML Characters

To prevent stored cross-site scripting attacks, you need to escape all dynamic content coming from a datastore so that the browser knows to treat it as the *content* of HTML tags, as opposed to raw HTML. *Escaping* content in the browser means replacing control characters in the HTML with their corresponding *entity encoding*, as illustrated in Table 7-1.

Table 7-1: Entity Encodings of HTML Control Characters

Character	Entity encoding
"	"
&	&
'	'
<	<
>	>

Any character that has special meaning in HTML, like the < and > characters that denote the start and end of tags, has a corresponding safe entity encoding. Browsers that encounter *entity encodings* recognize them as escaped characters, and render them visually as the appropriate character, but, crucially, won't treat them as HTML tags. Listing 7-1 shows how a secure website will write out the comment entered by the attack in Figure 7-1. The bolded text represents characters that could be used to construct HTML tags.

```
<div class="comment">
  &lt;script&gt;alert(&quot;HAXXED&quot;)&lt;/script&gt;
</div>
```

Listing 7-1: This attempted XSS attack has been defused.

The conversion of escaped characters to unescaped characters happens *after* the browser has constructed the DOM for the page, so the browser will *not* execute the <script> tag. Escaping HTML control characters in this fashion closes the door on most cross-site scripting attacks.

Since cross-site scripting is such a common vulnerability, modern web frameworks tend to escape dynamic content by default. Templates, in particular, typically escape interpolated values without being asked. The syntax for interpolating a variable in an *Embedded Ruby (ERB)* template looks like Listing 7-2.

```
<div class="comment">
  <%= comment %>
</div>
```

Listing 7-2: Implicit escaping of dynamic content in an Embedded Ruby template

The ERB templating engine will automatically escape sensitive characters via the <%= comment %> syntax when dynamic content is evaluated.

In order to write raw, unescaped HTML (and hence be vulnerable to XSS attacks), ERB templates require an explicit call to the raw function, as shown in Listing 7-3.

```
<div class="comment">
  <%= raw comment %>
</div>
```

Listing 7-3: The syntax to allow raw injection of HTML in Embedded Ruby templates

All secure templating languages follow the same design principle: the templating engine implicitly escapes dynamic content unless the developer explicitly chooses to construct raw HTML. Make sure you understand how escaping works in your templates, and check that dynamic content is securely escaped during code reviews! In particular, if you have helper functions or methods that construct raw HTML for injection into templates, check to see that an attacker can't abuse their inputs to commit cross-site scripting attacks.

Mitigation 2: Implement a Content Security Policy

Modern browsers allow websites to set a *content security policy*, which you can use to lock down JavaScript execution on your site. Cross-site scripting attacks rely on an attacker being able to run malicious scripts on a victim's web page, usually by injecting <script> tags somewhere within the <html> tag of a page, also known as *inline* JavaScript. The example hack illustrated in Figure 7-2 uses inline JavaScript, written out as the text of a comment.

By setting a content security policy in your HTTP response headers, you can tell the browser to *never* execute inline JavaScript. The browser will execute JavaScript on your page only if it is imported via a src attribute in the <script> tag. A typical content security policy header will look like Listing 7-4. This policy specifies that scripts can be imported from the same domain ('self'), or the *apis.google.com* domain, but inline JavaScript should not be executed.

```
Content-Security-Policy: script-src 'self' https://apis.google.com
```

Listing 7-4: A content security policy set in an HTTP response header

You can also set your site's content security policy in a <meta> tag in the <head> element of the HTML of your web pages, as shown in Listing 7-5.

```
<meta http-equiv="Content-Security-Policy" content="script-src 'self' https://apis.google.com">
```

Listing 7-5: The equivalent content security policy set in a <head> element of the HTML document

By whitelisting the domains from which your browser loads scripts, you implicitly state that inline JavaScript isn't allowed. In this example content security policy, the browser will load JavaScript only from the domains *apis .google.com* and whatever the domain of the site is—for example, *breddit.com*. To permit inline JavaScript, the policy would have to include the keyword unsafe-inline.

Preventing the execution of inline JavaScript is a great security measure, but it means you'll have to move any inline JavaScript your site currently implements into separate imports. In other words, <script> tags on a page have to reference JavaScript in a separate file via a src attribute, rather than writing the JavaScript between the start and end tags.

This separation of JavaScript into external files is the preferred approach in web development, since it makes for a more organized codebase. Inline script tags are considered bad practice in modern web development, so banning inline JavaScript actually forces your development team into good habits. Nevertheless, inline script tags are common in older, legacy sites. Indeed, it may take some time to refactor your templates to remove all inline JavaScript tags.

To help with this refactoring, consider using content security policy *violation reports*. If you add a `report-uri` directive to your content security policy header, as shown in Listing 7-6, the browser will notify you of any policy violations, rather than preventing JavaScript from executing.

```
Content-Security-Policy-Report-Only: script-src 'self'; report-uri https://example.com/csr-reports
```

Listing 7-6: A content security policy that instructs the browser to report any content security violations to https://example.com/csr-reports

If you collect all these violation reports in a log file, your development team should be able to see all the pages they need to rewrite in order to meet the restrictions imposed by the proposed content security policy.

You should set a content security policy in addition to escaping HTML, since it'll protect your users effectively! It's difficult for an attacker to find an instance of unescaped content *and* to smuggle a malicious script onto your whitelisted domains. We call using multiple layers of defense for the same vulnerability defense in depth, as you learned in Chapter 6; this will be a theme throughout this book.

Reflected Cross-Site Scripting Attacks

Rogue JavaScript in the database isn't the only vector for cross-site scripting attacks. If your site takes part of an HTTP request and displays it back in a rendered web page, your rendering code needs to protect against attacks that inject malicious JavaScript via the HTTP request. We call this type of attack a *reflected cross-site scripting* attack.

Virtually all websites display some part of HTTP requests in rendered HTML. Consider the Google search page: if you perform a search for "cats," Google passes the search term as part of the HTTP in the URL: *https://www.google.com/search?q=cats*. The search term cats displays in the search box above the search results.

Now, if Google were a less secure company, it'd be possible to replace the *cats* parameter in the URL with malicious JavaScript, and have that JavaScript code execute whenever anybody opens that URL in their browser. An attacker could email the URL as a link to a victim, or trick a user into visiting the URL by adding it to a comment. This is the essence of a *reflected* cross-site scripting attack: an attacker sends the malicious code in the HTML request, and then the server reflects it back.

Thankfully, Google employs more than a few security experts, so if you attempt to insert <script> tags into its search results, the server won't execute the JavaScript. In the past, hackers *have* discovered reflected cross-site scripting vulnerabilities in the Google Apps admin interface found at *https://admin.google.com*, so it goes to show that even big companies get caught out. If you want any chance of keeping your users safe, you need to protect against this attack vector.

Mitigation: Escape Dynamic Content from HTTP Requests

You mitigate reflected cross-site scripting vulnerabilities the same way you mitigate stored cross-site scripting vulnerabilities: by escaping control characters in dynamic content that the website interpolates into HTML pages. Whether dynamic content comes from the backend database or the HTTP request, you need to escape it in the same way.

Thankfully, template languages typically apply escaping to *all* interpolated variables, whether the templates load them from the database or pull them from the HTTP request. However, your development team still needs to be aware of the risk of injection via HTTP requests when auditing code. Code reviews often overlook reflected cross-site scripting vulnerabilities because developers are too busy looking for stored cross-site scripting vulnerabilities.

Common target areas for reflected cross-site scripting attacks are search pages and error pages, since they usually display parts of the query string back to the user. Make sure your team understands the risks and knows how to spot the vulnerability when reviewing code changes. Stored cross-site scripting attacks tend to be more harmful, because a single malicious piece of JavaScript injected into your database table can attack your users over and over again. But reflected attacks are more common, since they're easier to implement.

Before we close this chapter, let's look at one more type of cross-site scripting attack.

DOM-Based Cross-Site Scripting Attacks

Defusing most cross-site scripting attacks means inspecting and securing server-side code; however, the increasing popularity of rich frameworks for client-side code has led to the rise of *DOM-based cross-site scripting*, whereby attackers smuggle malicious JavaScript into a user's web page via the URI fragment.

To understand these attacks, you first need to understand how URI fragments operate. Let's start with a reminder of how *URLs (universal resource locators)*, the addresses shown in the browser bar, are structured. A typical URL looks like Figure 7-3.

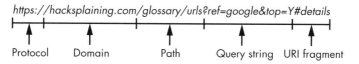

Figure 7-3: The sections of a typical URL

The URI fragment is the optional part of the URL after the # sign. Browsers use *URI fragments* for *intra-page* navigation—if an HTML tag on the page has an id attribute matching the URI fragment, the browser scrolls to that tag after opening the page. For instance, if you load the URL *https://en.wikipedia.org/wiki/Cat#Grooming* in a browser, the browser opens the web page and then scrolls to the Grooming section of the Wikipedia page about cats. It behaves this way because the heading tag for that section looks something like Listing 7-7.

```
<h3 id="Grooming">Grooming</h3>
```

Listing 7-7: An HTML tag corresponding to the URI fragment #Grooming

With this helpful built-in browser behavior, Wikipedia lets users link directly to sections within a page, so that you and your roommate can finally settle that contentious argument about cat grooming.

Single-page apps also often use URI fragments to record and reload state in an intuitive fashion. These types of apps, written in JavaScript frameworks like Angular, Vue.js, and React, are actually JavaScript-heavy web pages that seek to avoid the rendering *blink* that occurs when the browser reloads a web page.

One potential way to avoid this rendering blink is designing the whole app to load under a static URL that never changes, because changing the URL in the browser bar is typically what causes a web page to reload. However, if a user refreshes a browser for an unchanging URL, the browser resets the web page to its initial state, losing any information about what the user was doing previously.

Many single-page apps overcome this by using the URI fragment to keep state over browser refreshes. You'll commonly see web pages implement *infinite scrolling*: a list of images dynamically loads in as the user scrolls down the page. The URI fragment updates with an indication of how far the user has scrolled down. Then, even if the browser refreshes, the JavaScript code can interpret the content of the URI fragment, and load in the relevant number of images as the page refreshes.

By design, browsers don't send URI fragments to the server when the browser renders the page. When a browser receives a URL with a URI fragment, it makes a note of the fragment, strips it from the URL, and sends the stripped URL to the web server. Any JavaScript executed on the page can read the URI fragment, and the browser will write the full URL to the browser history, or to a bookmark, if the user bookmarks the page.

Unfortunately, this means that URI fragments aren't available to any server-side code—securing server-side code *can't* mitigate DOM-based XSS attacks. Client-side JavaScript code that interprets and uses URI fragments needs to be careful about how it interprets the content of those fragments. If the content is unescaped and written directly into the DOM of the web page, an attacker can smuggle malicious JavaScript through this channel. An attacker can craft a URL with some malicious JavaScript in the URI fragment, and then trick a user into visiting that URL to launch the cross-site scripting attack.

DOM-based cross-site scripting is a relatively new form of attack, but is particularly dangerous because the injection of code happens completely on the client side, and can't be detected by examining web server logs! This means you need to be keenly aware of the vulnerability when doing code reviews, and know how to mitigate it.

Mitigation: Escaping Dynamic Content from URI Fragments

Any JavaScript code executing in the browser that takes part of the URI fragment and constructs HTML is prone to DOM-based cross-site scripting attacks. This means you need to take care to *escape* anything taken from a URI fragment before interpolating that value in HTML with the client-side code, just as you would with server-side code.

The authors of modern JavaScript templating frameworks are fully aware of the risks posed by URI fragments and discourage the construction of raw HTML in code. For instance, the syntax to write unescaped HTML in the React framework requires the developer to call the function dangerously SetInnerHTML, as shown in Listing 7-8.

```
function writeSomeHTML () {
  return {__html: 'First &middot; Second'};
}
function MyComponent() {
  return <div dangerouslySetInnerHTML={writeSomeHTML()} />;
}
```

Listing 7-8: Dangerously setting raw HTML from text in the React framework

Consider switching to a modern JavaScript framework if your client-side JavaScript code is complex. It should make the codebase more manageable and security considerations much more apparent. And as always, be sure to set an appropriate content security policy.

Summary

In this chapter, you learned about cross-site scripting attacks, whereby an attacker injects JavaScript into the pages of your site when users view them. Attackers usually inject malicious JavaScript into dynamic content that comes from a database, from the HTTP request, or from the URI fragment. You can defeat cross-site scripting attacks by escaping any HTML control characters in dynamic content, and by setting a content security policy that prevents the execution of inline JavaScript.

In the next chapter, you'll look at another method that attackers can use to prey on the users of your website: cross-site request forgery.

8

CROSS-SITE REQUEST FORGERY ATTACKS

In the previous chapter, you saw how attackers use cross-site scripting attacks to inject JavaScript into a user's web browser through page elements like comment sections, search results, and URLs. Now you'll look at how attackers use malicious links to hack your users.

No website is an island. Because your website has a public URL, other sites will frequently link to it, which you should generally encourage as a site owner. More inbound links to your site means more traffic and better search engine rankings.

However, not everybody linking to your site has good intentions. An attacker can trick a user into clicking a malicious link that triggers undesirable or unexpected side effects. This is called *cross-site request forgery (CSRF or XSRF)*. Security researchers sometimes pronounce CSRF as "sea-surf."

CSRF is a remarkably common vulnerability that most major websites have exhibited at one time or another. Attackers have used CSRF to steal

Gmail contact lists, trigger one-click purchases on Amazon, and change router configuration. This chapter examines how CSRF attacks typically work and shows some coding practices that protect against them.

Anatomy of a CSRF Attack

Attackers usually launch CSRF attacks by exploiting websites that implement GET requests that change the state of a web server. A GET request is triggered when a victim clicks a link, allowing the attacker to craft misleading links into the target site that perform unexpected actions. GET requests are the only type of HTTP request that contain the entirety of the request's contents in a URL, so they're uniquely vulnerable to CSRF attacks.

In an early iteration of Twitter, you could create tweets via GET requests rather than the POST requests the site currently uses. This oversight made Twitter vulnerable to CSRF attacks: it made it possible to create URL links that, when clicked, would post on a user's timeline. Listing 8-1 shows one of these URL links.

```
https://twitter.com/share/update?status=in%20ur%20twitter%20CSRF-ing%20ur%20tweets
```

Listing 8-1: A link that, at one point, would have tweeted the text in ur twitter CSRF-ing ur tweets to a victim's timeline when clicked

One canny hacker used this loophole to create a viral *worm* on Twitter. Because they could use a single GET request to write a tweet, they constructed a malicious link that, when clicked, would post a tweet containing an obscene message *and* the same malicious link. When readers of the tweet clicked the link that the first victim tweeted, they too were tricked into tweeting the same thing.

The hacker tricked a handful of victims into clicking the malicious link, and those victims tweeted unexpected posts on the timelines. As more and more users read the original tweets and clicked the embedded link out of curiosity, they too tweeted the same thing. Soon, tens of thousands of Twitter users were being tricked into expressing their desire to molest goats (the content of the initial tweet). The first Twitter worm was born, and the Twitter development team scrambled to close the security hole before things got out of hand.

Mitigation 1: Follow REST Principles

To protect your users against CSRF attacks, make sure that your GET requests don't change the state of the server. Your website should use GET requests only to fetch web pages or other resources. You should perform actions that change server state—for example, logging the user in or out, resetting passwords, writing posts, or closing an account—only through PUT, POST, or DELETE requests. This design philosophy, called *Representational State Transfer (REST)*, comes with a host of other benefits besides CSRF protection.

REST states that you should map website operations to the appropriate HTTP method according to their intention. You should fetch data or pages with `GET` requests, create new objects on the server (such as comments, uploads, or messages) with `PUT` requests, modify objects on the server with `POST` requests, and delete objects with `DELETE` requests.

Not all actions have an obvious corresponding HTTP method. For instance, when a user logs in, it's a philosophical discussion as to whether the user is creating a new session or modifying their status. In terms of protecting against CSRF attacks, though, the key thing is to avoid assigning actions that change the server state to `GET` requests.

Protecting your `GET` requests doesn't mean that there aren't vulnerabilities in other types of requests, as you'll see with our second mitigation.

Mitigation 2: Implement Anti-CSRF Cookies

Defusing your `GET` requests shuts the door on most CSRF attacks, but you still need to protect against requests using the other HTTP verbs. Attacks using those verbs are much less common than `GET`-based CSRF attacks, and require much more work, but an attacker might try them if they think the payoff is sufficient.

For instance, they can trick a user into initiating a `POST` request to your site by having the victim submit a malicious form or script hosted on a third-party site under the attacker's control. If your site performs sensitive actions in response to `POST` requests, you need to use anti-CSRF cookies to ensure that these requests are initiated only from within your site. Sensitive actions should be triggered only from your own login forms and JavaScript, rather than malicious pages that may trick the user into performing unexpected actions.

An *anti-CSRF cookie* is a randomized string token that the web server writes out to a named cookie parameter. Recall that cookies are small pieces of text passed back and forth between the browser and web server in HTTP headers. If the web server returns an HTTP response containing a header value like `Set-Cookie: _xsrf=5978e29d4ef434a1`, the browser will send back the same information in the next HTTP request in a header with form `Cookie: _xsrf=5978e29d4ef434a1`.

Secure websites use anti-CSRF cookies to verify that `POST` requests originate from pages hosted on the same web domain. HTML pages on the site add this same string token as an `<input type="hidden" name="_xsrf" value="5978e29d4ef434a1">` element in any HTML form used to generate `POST` requests. When a user submits the form to the server, and the `_xsrf` value in the returned cookie doesn't match the `_xsrf` value in the request body, the server rejects the request entirely. This way, the server validates and ensures that the request originated from within the site rather than from a malicious third-party site; the browser will send the required cookie *only* when the web page is loaded from the same domain.

Most modern web servers support anti-CSRF cookies. Make sure to consult the security documentation of your chosen web server to understand how they implement these cookies, since the syntax varies slightly among web servers. Listing 8-2 shows a template file for the Tornado web server that includes anti-CSRF protection.

```
<form action="/new_message" method="post">
❶ {% module xsrf_form_html() %}
  <input type="text" name="message"/>
  <input type="submit" value="Post"/>
</form>
```

Listing 8-2: A template file for the Tornado web server in Python that includes anti-CSRF protection

In this example, the xsrf_form_html() function ❶ generates a randomized token and writes it out in the HTML form as an input element like so: `<input type="hidden" name="_xsrf" value="5978e29d4ef434a1">`. The Tornado web server then writes out this same token in the HTTP response headers as `Set-Cookie: _xsrf=5978e29d4ef434a1`. When the user submits the form, the web server validates that the token from the form and the token in the return Cookie header match. The browser security model will return cookies according to the *same-origin policy*, so the cookie values can only have been set by the web server. Hence the server can be sure that the POST request originated from the host website.

You should use anti-CSRF cookies to validate HTTP requests made from JavaScript, too, which allows you to also protect PUT and DELETE requests. The JavaScript needs to query out the anti-CSRF token from the HTML, and pass it back to the server in the HTTP request.

After you've implemented anti-CSRF cookies, your website should be much safer. Now you need to close one final loophole, to make sure attackers can't steal your anti-CSRF tokens and embed them in malicious code.

Mitigation 3: Use the SameSite Cookie Attribute

The final protection against CSRF attacks you must implement is to specify a SameSite attribute when you set cookies. By default, when a browser generates a request to your website, it will attach to the request the last known cookies that the site set, regardless of the source of the request. This means that malicious cross-site requests will arrive at your web server with any security cookies you previously set. This doesn't defeat anti-CSRF measures in and of itself, but if an attacker steals the security token from your HTML forms, and installs it in their own malicious forms, they can still launch a CSRF attack.

Specifying a SameSite attribute when you set a cookie tells the browser to strip cookies on a request to your site when the request is generated from an external domain—like a malicious website set up by an attacker. Setting a cookie with the SameSite=Strict syntax in Listing 8-3 ensures that the browser will send the cookie only with requests initiated from within your own site.

```
Set-Cookie: _xsrf=5978e29d4ef434a1; SameSite=Strict;
```

Listing 8-3: Setting the SameSite attribute to our anti-CSRF cookie ensures that the cookie attaches to only requests from our site.

It's a good idea to set a SameSite attribute on all your cookies, not just those used for CSRF protection. There's a caveat to this, however: if you use cookies for session management, setting the SameSite attribute to your session cookie strips the cookie of any requests to your site generated from other websites. This means that any inbound links to your site will force the user to log in again.

This behavior can be a little annoying for users who already have a session open on your site. Imagine if you had to log back into Facebook every time somebody shared a video. Frustrating, right? To prevent this behavior, Listing 8-4 shows a more useful value of the SameSite attribute, Lax, that allows only GET requests from other sites to send cookies.

```
Set-Cookie: session_id=82938d911e13f3; SameSite=Lax;
```

Listing 8-4: Setting the SameSite attribute on an HTTP cookie allows cookies on GET requests.

This allows seamless linking into your site, but strips the ability of an attacker to forge malicious actions such as POST requests. Provided your GET requests are side-effect free, this setting is no less safe.

Bonus Mitigation: Require Reauthentication for Sensitive Actions

You might notice that some websites force you to reconfirm your login details when you perform sensitive actions, such as when you change your password or initiate a payment. This is known as *reauthentication*, and it's a common way to secure sites against CSRF attacks, because it gives the user a clear indication that you're about to do something significant and potentially dangerous.

Reauthentication also has the positive side effect of protecting your users if they accidentally leave themselves logged in on shared or stolen devices. If your website handles financial transactions or confidential data, you should strongly consider forcing your users to reenter their credentials when they perform sensitive actions.

Summary

Attackers can use web requests from other sites to trick your users into performing undesired actions. The solution to such cross-site request forgery attacks is threefold.

First, make sure your GET requests are side-effect free, so the server state is not changed when a user clicks malicious links. Second, use anti-CSRF cookies to protect other types of requests. Third, set these cookies with a SameSite attribute to strip cookies from requests generated by other sites.

For very sensitive actions on your site, it's a good idea to require the user to reauthenticate themselves when they request to perform these actions. This adds an additional layer of protection against CSRF attacks, and protects your users if they accidentally leave themselves logged in on shared or stolen devices.

In the next chapter, you'll look at how hackers try to exploit vulnerabilities during the authentication process.

9

COMPROMISING AUTHENTICATION

 Most websites provide some sort of login functionality. This is a form of *authentication*, the process of identifying users when they return to your website. Authenticating your users allows them to have an identity in an online community where they can contribute content, send messages to others, make purchases, and so on.

Nowadays, internet users are comfortable with signing up to a site with a username and password, and logging back in when they next want to use it. This is especially true since browsers and plug-ins help with caching or choosing passwords, and third-party authentication services have become ubiquitous.

There's a downside to this, however. Getting access to a user's account is a tantalizing prospect for hackers. In the age of the internet, it has never been easier for hackers to sell hacked credentials on the dark web, hijack social media accounts to spread clickbait, and commit financial fraud.

In this chapter, you'll investigate some of the ways that hackers can compromise a user's account on your site during the login and authentication process. (The next chapter covers the vulnerabilities your users face after they've logged in and established a session.) Here, you'll first see the most common ways websites implement authentication and look at how attackers use brute-force attacks to exploit them. Then you'll learn how to protect users against these attacks through third-party authentication, single sign-on, and securing your own authentication system.

Implementing Authentication

Authentication is part of the HyperText Transfer Protocol. To present an authentication challenge, a web server needs to return a 401 status code in the HTTP response and add a `WWW-Authenticate` header describing the preferred authentication method. (There are two commonly supported authentication methods: basic authentication and digest authentication.) To fulfill this requirement, the user agent—usually a web browser—needs to request a username and password from the user, thus creating the login functionality.

In the *basic authentication* scheme, the browser concatenates the username and password supplied by the user with a colon (:) character between them, generating the string *username:password*. It then uses the Base64 algorithm to encode this string and send it back to the server in the `Authorization` header of an HTTP request.

The *digest authentication* scheme is a little more complex, and requires the browser to generate a hash consisting of the username, password, and URL. A *hash* is the output of a one-way encryption algorithm that makes it easy to generate a unique "fingerprint" for a set of input data, but makes it difficult to guess the input values if you have only the algorithm's output. You'll look at hashing in more depth later in this chapter, when we discuss how to securely store passwords.

HTTP-Native Authentication

Even though authentication is built into the HyperText Transfer Protocol, popular websites rarely use basic or digest authentication—mostly because of usability considerations. The native web browser authentication prompt is *not* a thing of beauty. It looks similar to a JavaScript alert dialog, grabbing focus from the browser, and interrupting the experience of using the site, as shown in Figure 9-1.

Because browsers implement the authentication prompt outside HTML, we can't style the native authentication prompt to match the website. As a native browser window that doesn't appear in the web page, the browser also can't autocomplete the user's credentials. Finally, because HTTP authentication specifies no method of resetting a password if a user forgets it, we'd have to implement a reset feature separately from the login prompt, leading to a confusing user experience.

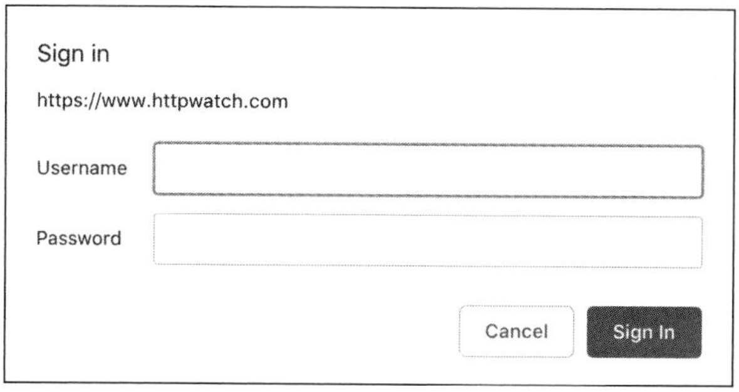

Figure 9-1: The native Google Chrome login prompt rudely interrupts your browsing session.

Non-Native Authentication

Because of this user-hostile design, the built-in HTTP authentication methods tend to be reserved mostly for applications where the user experience simply doesn't matter that much. Modern websites usually implement their own login forms in HTML, like the one shown in Listing 9-1.

```
<form action="/login" method="post">
❶ <input type="email" name="username" placeholder="Type your email">
❷ <input type="password" name="password" placeholder="Type your password">
   <input type="submit" name="login" value="Log in">
</form>
```

Listing 9-1: A typical login form in HTML

A typical login form contains an `<input type="text">` element ❶ requiring the user to supply a username, and an `<input type="password">` element ❷ that replaces typed characters with a • character to obscure the password. The supplied username and password are sent to the server as a POST request when the user submits the form. If the login is unsuccessful because the user couldn't be authenticated, the server replies with a 401 status code in the HTTP response. If the login is successful, the server redirects the user to their homepage.

Brute-Force Attacks

Attackers often attempt to compromise your site at the point of authentication by guessing passwords. Movies usually depict hackers using personal insights about a target to guess their password. While this might be a concern for high-profile targets, hackers usually have more success using *brute-force attacks*, which use scripts to try thousands of commonly used passwords against a login page. Because previous data breaches have already leaked millions of commonly used passwords, including the ones in Listing 9-2, it's easy for an attacker to determine which passwords they should try first.

1. 123456
2. password
3. 12345678
4. qwerty
5. 12345
6. 123456789
7. letmein
8. 1234567
9. football
10. iloveyou

Listing 9-2: Security researchers publish a list of the most commonly used passwords each year; they change very little year to year. (This list is provided by the internet security firm SplashData.)

Let's look at a few ways you can implement and secure your authentication against this type of threat.

Mitigation 1: Use Third-Party Authentication

The most secure authentication system is the one you don't have to write yourself. Instead of implementing your own authentication system, consider using a third-party service like Facebook Login, which allows users to authenticate to your website with their social media credentials. This is convenient for them, and relieves you of the burden of ever having to store user passwords.

Large tech companies provide other similar authentication services. Most of them are based on the *open authentication (OAuth)* or *OpenID* standards—commonly implemented protocols for delegating authentication to a third party. You can always mix and match authentication systems. They're typically straightforward to integrate with, so pick one or more that make sense with your userbase. If you're providing email-related services, you can integrate with Google OAuth to ask your users for access to their Gmail accounts. If you're providing technical services, use something like GitHub OAuth. Twitter, Microsoft, LinkedIn, Reddit, and Tumblr all offer authentication options, as do hundreds of other websites.

Mitigation 2: Integrate with Single Sign-On

If you integrate with an OAuth or OpenID identity provider, your users will usually use their personal email addresses as usernames. However, if your website's target audience is business users, consider integrating with a *single sign-on (SSO)* identity provider like Okta, OneLogin, or Centrify, which centralizes authentication across enterprise systems so employees can log in seamlessly to third-party applications under their business email. Company administrators retain ultimate control over which employees can access what sites, and user credentials are stored securely on the company's servers.

To integrate with a single sign-on provider, you'll usually have to use *Security Assertion Markup Language (SAML),* which is an older (and less friendly) standard than OAuth or OpenID, though most programming languages have mature SAML libraries you can use.

Mitigation 3: Secure Your Own Authentication System

Although third-party authentication will usually be more secure than your own system, having only third-party authentication could somewhat limit your userbase because not everyone has a social media presence or Gmail account. For everyone else, you'll need to create a way for them to sign up and manually choose a username and password. This means creating separate pages on your website where users can sign up, log in, and log out; plus writing code to store and update credentials in your database, and to check that the credentials are correct when a user reenters them. More than likely, you will need to have a mechanism for a user to change their password too.

That's a lot of functionality to implement! Before you start writing code, you'll need to make a few design decisions. Let's look at the key things you need to get right in order to have a secure authentication system.

Requiring Usernames, Email Address, or Both

Your users will need to choose a username and password when they sign up. Most websites will also require a user to submit a valid email address when they sign up, which allows them to send password-reset emails when users forget their credentials.

For many sites, a user's email address *is* their username. By necessity, each email address has to be unique to an account, so choosing a separate username would generally be redundant. The exception to this is when users have a visible presence on the site; for example, when a user has a public profile, or interacts with other users in comment sections. These types of sites require users to choose a separate *display name.* Using email addresses as display names is bad practice, since it invites harassment and spam.

Validating Email Addresses

If you intend to send email from your site—for instance, to allow users to reset their password—you need to validate that every user's email address corresponds to a working email account. Emails that a website generates are called *transactional emails,* because the website sends them in response to a user action. Sending transactional emails to unverified addresses will quickly get you blacklisted by your email service provider, since they're wary of enabling spammers.

First, verify that the user's email address appears valid on its face. This means validating that the email contains only valid characters: letters, numbers, or any of the special characters (!#$%&'*+-/=?^_`{|}~;.).

The address must contain an @ sign, and to the right of that, a valid internet domain. Usually, but not always, this domain should correspond to a website, like *@gmail.com* addresses that correspond to *www.gmail.com*. At a minimum, the internet's *Domain Name System (DNS)*, which we discussed in Chapter 2, must contain a mail exchange (MX) record for that domain that tells software where to route emails. It's possible to look up the MX record as part of your verification process, as shown in Listing 9-3.

```
import dns.resolver
def email_domain_is_valid(domain):
  for _ in dns.resolver.query(domain, 'MX'):
    return True
  return False
```

Listing 9-3: Validating that a domain is capable of receiving email in Python by using the dnsresolver library

However, the only 100 percent reliable way to validate that an address corresponds to a working email account is to send an email message and check that it's received. This means you'll have to send each user an email that contains an *email verification link* that links back to your website and contains a *validation token*—a large, randomly generated string you store in your database against their email address. When the user clicks the link to verify ownership of their email address, you can check that the validation token is the one you sent out, and confirm that they do indeed have access to the email account.

Many sites force users to validate their email before they can complete the sign-up process. Other sites allow the user to use a limited number of features on the site while they're in an unvalidated state, in order to make the sign-up process less onerous. You should never assume a user has access to an email account until you've validated them. Until then, don't send any other types of transactional email or sign the user up to mailing lists!

Banning Disposable Email Accounts

Some users are reluctant to sign up with an email address they commonly use, and will sign up to your site using a temporary email account generated by services like 10 Minute Mail or Mailinator or the one shown in Figure 9-2. These types of services generate a disposable email account that's good for receiving a handful of messages before shutting down. If a user uses this type of service, it usually means they're wary of being signed up to mailing lists (quite a reasonable consideration, given the relentless approach of email marketers).

You may need to ban users from signing up with disposable email addresses if, for instance, some of your users are generating temporary accounts to harass others. If so, you can use well-maintained blacklists of disposable email providers to detect, reject, and ban disposable email domains during the sign-up process.

Figure 9-2: Want a temporary email address? Come get it at https://www.sharklasers.com/. (Yes, this is a real website. Pew pew pew.)

Securing Password Resets

Having a validated email address for each of your users allows you to handle the (inevitable) scenario when a user forgets their password. Simply send them an email with a *password-reset link*, containing a fresh validation token. When the forgetful user opens the email and clicks the link, you can validate the incoming token, and allow the user to choose a new password for their account.

Password-reset links should be short-lived, and should expire after the user uses them. A good rule of thumb is to expire reset tokens after 30 minutes to prevent an attacker from abusing stale reset links. If an attacker hacks a user's email account, you can't let them search for emails containing reset links and then use those links to access your site under the victim's account.

Requiring Complex Passwords

Complex passwords are generally harder to guess, so you should require users to meet certain password complexity standards when they choose a password, for their own protection. Complex passwords include numbers and symbols as well as letters, have a mix of uppercase and lowercase characters, and are long rather than short. At the very least, you should enforce a minimum length of eight characters for passwords, but the longer the better. (Studies have shown that password length is more important than mixing in unusual characters.)

However, users often have trouble remembering complex passwords, so if you enforce overly strict password complexity requirements, a user will usually reuse a password they previously entered on another website. Some secure sites prevent a user from reusing a password they previously used to force them to choose a new, unique password each time, pushing them away from lazy habits. Unfortunately, most users will simply cycle passwords by adding a number at the end of a password they commonly use, which doesn't make for a significantly less guessable password.

Ultimately, each user is responsible for their own security online, so it's generally better to nudge your users toward strong password choices rather than forcing them to jump through hoops. Some JavaScript libraries, like the `password-strength-calculator` library, can be used to rate a user's password's complexity as they type it and to call out commonly used passwords, which you can use on sign-up and password-reset screens to push users toward a more secure password.

Securely Storing Passwords

After a user chooses a password, you need to record it in some form in your database against their username, so you can revalidate their credentials when they log in again. Do *not* simply store the password as is—we call this *cleartext* storage, and it's a big security no-no. If an attacker accesses a database that stores passwords in cleartext form, they can compromise every user account, as well as accounts those users have on other websites under the same credentials. Luckily, there is a way of storing passwords in a secure fashion that makes them unreadable in the database, but allows you to check they have been reentered correctly by a user at a later date.

Hashing Passwords

Passwords should be processed with a *cryptographic hash algorithm* before being stored in your database. This will convert the raw string of input text into a bit string of fixed length in such a way that makes it computationally unfeasible to reverse the process. You should then store the output values of that algorithm—the *hashed values*—alongside each username.

Hashing algorithms are a type of one-way mathematical function. The only practical way to guess the input string that generated a given hashed output (or *hash*, for short) is to try every possible input string one after the other. By storing a hash of a user's password, you can recalculate the hash when a user reenters their password and compare the new and old hash values to see if they've entered the correct password.

Numerous cryptographic hash algorithms exist, each with varying implementations and strengths. A good hashing algorithm should be quick to calculate, but not *too* quick. Otherwise, as computation speeds increase, brute-force attempts to crack the password by enumerating all possible inputs become feasible. For this reason, a good algorithm to use is *bcrypt*, shown in Listing 9-4, which allows you to add extra iterations to the hashing function as the years go by to make it stronger and more time-consuming as computation power gets cheaper.

```
import bcrypt
password = "super secret password"

# Hash a password for the first time, with a randomly-generated salt
hashed = bcrypt.hashpw(password, bcrypt.gensalt(rounds=14❶))

# Check that an unhashed password matches one that has previously been hashed
if bcrypt.checkpw(password, hashed):
    print("It matches!")
else:
    print("It does not match :(")
```

Listing 9-4: Hashing and then testing a password using the bcrypt algorithm in Python

The rounds parameter at ❶ can be incremented to make the password hashes even stronger. Storing hashed passwords rather than cleartext passwords is much more secure. No one who accesses the database, including you, can directly decipher the passwords, but your website can still determine whether a user has correctly reentered their password. This relieves you of a security burden—even if an attacker hacks your database, they can't do much with the hashed passwords.

Salting Hashes

Hashing passwords makes your site more secure, but users are frequently unimaginative in their password choice. When *cracking* password lists—reverse engineering passwords for a list of leaked password hashes—hackers frequently use *rainbow tables*, which are lists of commonly used passwords that have been put through a known hashing algorithm. Matching hashes against precalculated values yield a very good return for an attacker, allowing them to determine the password for many, if not most, of the hashes.

To protect against rainbow table attacks, you need to *salt* your password hashes, which means adding an element of randomness to the hashing algorithm so the input password doesn't solely determine the generated hash. You can store the salt input value in your configuration, or better yet, generate a salt input value separately for each user and store it alongside their password hash. This makes rainbow table attacks unfeasible, since an attacker has to regenerate the entire rainbow table for each salt value you use, which is computationally prohibitive and thus takes too long.

Requiring Multifactor Authentication

No matter how securely you store passwords, password-based authentication systems are always vulnerable to brute-force password-guessing attacks. To really secure your website, consider adding an extra layer of security by requiring *multifactor authentication (MFA)*, which requires a returning user to identify themselves with at least two of the following three categories of information: something they *know*, something they *have*, and something they *are*. One example of multifactor authentication is a bank ATM, which requires the account holder's PIN (the thing they know) and their bank card (the thing they have). Another example would be devices that use biometrics to identify individuals, like fingerprint scanning on smartphones (the thing they are).

For websites, multifactor authentication generally boils down to requiring a username and password (the thing the user knows), and confirming that the user has an authenticator installed on their smartphone (the thing they have). Each user will need to sync the authenticator app with the website during sign up (usually by taking a photograph of a QR code onscreen.) Thereafter, the app generates a six-digit random number that they need to supply at login time for the user to log in successfully, like the one shown in Figure 9-3.

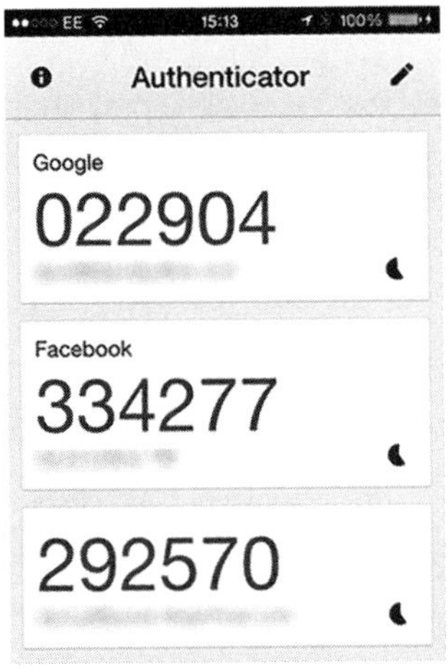

Figure 9-3: Your users will come to love typing in six-digit numbers.

This forces an attacker to have knowledge of a victim's credentials *and* access to the victim's smartphone in order to compromise their account, which is a highly unlikely combination. Support for multifactor authentication is increasingly becoming the norm, given the ubiquity of smartphones. If your website does any type of financial processing, you should definitely implement multifactor authentication. Thankfully, many code libraries make integrating it relatively easy.

Implementing and Securing the Logout Function

If you authenticate users on your site, don't forget to add a function that lets them log out of your site too. This might seem like an anachronism, given that users seem to stay perpetually logged in to social media, but having a logout function is a key security consideration for users who log in on shared devices. Plenty of families share a laptop or iPad, and companies often reuse computers and portable devices, so make sure to let your users log out!

Your logout function should clear the session cookie in the browser, *and* invalidate the session identifier if you are storing it on the server side. This protects against attackers who manage to intercept session cookies after the fact and attempt to reestablish a session using a stolen cookie. Clearing the session cookie is as simple as sending back an HTTP response containing a Set-Cookie header with a blank value for your session parameter.

Preventing User Enumeration

You can cut down the risk of an attacker compromising your authentication system if they can't *enumerate* users, which means testing each username from a list to see whether it exists on your website. Attackers frequently use leaked credentials from prior hacks and attempt to verify whether any of these usernames exist on a target website. After they narrow down the list, they then proceed to guess passwords for usernames that matched.

Preventing Potential Enumeration Vulnerabilities

Login pages often allow an attacker to determine whether a username is taken on a site. If the page shows an error message for an incorrect password that differs from the error message for an unknown user, then an attacker can infer from the responses whether certain usernames correspond to accounts that exist on your site. It's important to keep the error messages generic to avoid leaking this type of information. For example, simply use the error message an incorrect username or password was entered whenever the username is unrecognized or the password is incorrect.

Attackers may also use *timing attacks* to enumerate users by measuring HTTP response times. Hashing a password is a time-consuming operation; though it typically takes less than a second, it's still a measurable amount of time. If your site calculates password hashes only when a user enters a valid username, an attacker can measure the slightly slower response time to infer which accounts exist on the site. Make sure your site calculates password hashes during authentication even for invalid usernames.

You should prevent your password-reset screen from revealing that a username exists, too. If an attacker clicks a "Forgotten password" link and types in an email address to request a password-reset link, the response message on the page shouldn't reveal whether a reset email was sent. This prevents the attacker from knowing whether that email address is tied to an account on your site. Keep the message neutral: something like Check your inbox.

Implementing CAPTCHA

You can also defuse user enumeration attacks by implementing a *CAPTCHA (Completely Automated Public Turing test to tell Computers and Humans Apart)*, which asks web users to perform various image recognition tasks that are trivial for humans but tricky for computers. CAPTCHAs, like the one shown in Figure 9-4, make it impractical for attackers to abuse a web page via hacking scripts.

CAPTCHAs aren't perfect. Attackers can defeat them by using sophisticated machine learning techniques, or by paying human users to complete a task in their stead. However, they are generally reliable enough to deter most hacking attempts, and you can easily add them to a website. For example, Google implements a CAPTCHA widget called reCAPTCHA that you can install on your site with a few lines of code.

Figure 9-4: Some tasks are simply too hard for a computer to complete successfully.

Summary

Hackers often attempt to attack your authentication system in an effort to steal your users' credentials. To secure your website, you can use a third-party authentication system like Facebook Login or a single sign-on identity provider.

If you're implementing your own authentication system, you'll need to have users choose a username and password upon sign-up. You should also store and validate an email address for each user. It makes sense to use this email as a username, unless you need users to have a visible display name.

The only reliable way to validate an email address is to send it an email containing a link with a unique, temporary validation token that your site can check when the user clicks it. Your password-reset mechanism for users who have forgotten their password should work in the same way. Password-reset emails and the initial validation email should time out after a period of time, and after they're used for the first time.

You should process passwords with a cryptographic hash algorithm before storing them. You should also salt your password hashes to prevent rainbow table attacks.

Consider adding multifactor authentication if your site hosts sensitive data. Make sure to include a logout function somewhere on your site. Keep login failure messages generic, to prevent hackers from enumerating usernames on your site.

In the next chapter, you will investigate ways that users on your site can have their account compromised after they log in, by having their session stolen by an attacker.

10

SESSION HIJACKING

When a website successfully authenticates a user, the browser and the server open a session. A *session* is an HTTP conversation in which the browser sends a series of HTTP requests corresponding to user actions, and the web server recognizes them as coming from the same authenticated user without requiring the user to log back in for each request.

If a hacker can access or forge session information that the browser sends, they can access any user's account on your site. Thankfully, modern web servers contain secure session-management code, which makes it practically impossible for an attacker to manipulate or forge a session. However, even if there are no vulnerabilities in a server's session-management capabilities, a hacker can still steal someone else's valid session while it's in progress; this is called *session hijacking*.

Session hijacking vulnerabilities are generally a bigger risk than the authentication vulnerabilities discussed in the previous chapter, because again, they allow an attacker to access any of your users' accounts. This is such a tantalizing prospect that hackers have found many ways to hijack sessions.

In this chapter, you'll first look at how websites implement session management. Then you'll learn about the three ways hackers hijack sessions: cookie theft, session fixation, and taking advantage of weak session IDs.

How Sessions Work

To understand how an attacker hijacks a session, you first need to understand what happens when a user and a web server open a session.

When a user authenticates themselves under HTTP, the web server assigns them a session identifier during the login process. The *session identifier (session ID)*—typically a large, randomly generated number—is the minimal information the browser needs to transmit with each subsequent HTTP request so the server can continue the HTTP conversation with the authenticated user. The web server recognizes the session ID supplied with each request, maps it to the appropriate user, and performs actions on their behalf.

Note that the session ID must be a temporarily assigned value that's different from the username. If the browser used a session ID that was simply the username, hackers could pretend to be any user they pleased. By design, only a very small minority of possible session IDs should correspond to a valid session on the server at any given time. (If this is not the case, the web server exhibits a weak session vulnerability, which we will discuss later in this chapter.)

Besides the username, the web server typically stores other *session state* alongside the session ID, containing relevant information about the user's recent activity. The session state might, for example, contain a list of pages the user has visited, or the items currently sitting in their shopping basket.

Now that we understand what happens when users and web servers open a session, let's look at how websites implement these sessions. There are two common implementations, typically described as server-side sessions and client-side sessions. Let's review how these methods work, so you can see where the vulnerabilities occur.

Server-Side Sessions

In a traditional model of session management, the web server keeps the session state in memory, and both the web server and browser pass the session identifier back and forth. This is called a *server-side session*. Listing 10-1 shows the Ruby on Rails implementation of server-side sessions.

```
# Get a session from the cache.
def find_session(env, sid)
  unless sid && (session = @cache.read(cache_key(sid))❶)
```

```
      sid, session = generate_sid❷, {}
    end
    [sid, session]
  end

  # Set a session in the cache.
  def write_session(env, sid, session, options)
    key = cache_key(sid)
    if session
❸   @cache.write(key, session, expires_in: options[:expire_after])
    else
      @cache.delete(key)
    end
    sid
  end
end
```

Listing 10-1: Ruby on Rails implements server-side sessions using the session ID (sid).

The session object is created at ❷, written to the server's memory at ❸, and then reloaded from memory at ❶.

Historically, web servers have experimented with transferring session IDs in multiple ways: either in the URL, as an HTTP header, or in the body of HTTP requests. By far, the most common (and reliable) mechanism the web development community has decided upon is to send session IDs as a session cookie. When using *session cookies*, the web server returns the session ID in the Set-Cookie header of the HTTP response, and the browser attaches the same information to subsequent HTTP requests using the Cookie header.

Cookies have been part of the HyperText Transfer Protocol since they were first introduced by Netscape in 1995. Unlike HTTP-native authentication, they're used by pretty much every website under the sun. (Because of European Union legislation, you'll be well aware of this fact: websites are required by European law to inform you that they're using cookies.)

Server-side sessions have been widely implemented and are generally very secure. They do have scalability limitations, however, because the web server has to store the session state in memory.

That means that at authentication time, only *one* of the web servers will know about the established session. If subsequent web requests for the same user gets directed to a *different* web server, the new web server needs to be able to recognize the returning user, so web servers need a way of sharing session information.

Typically, this requires writing session state to a shared cache or to a database with every request, and having each web server read that cached session state when a new HTTP request comes through. Both of these are time- and resource-consuming operations that can limit the responsiveness of sites with large userbases, since each user added to the website adds a significant load to the session store.

Client-Side Sessions

Because server-side sessions have proven difficult to scale for large sites, web server developers invented client-side sessions. A web server implementing *client-side sessions* passes all session state in the cookie, instead of passing back just the session ID in the Set-Cookie header. The server serializes session state to text before the session state is set in the HTTP header. Often, web servers encode the session state as JavaScript Object Notation (JSON)—and deserialize it when returning it to the server. Listing 10-2 shows an example of Ruby on Rails implementing a client-side session.

```
def set_cookie(request, session_id, cookie)
  cookie_jar(request)[@key] = cookie
end

def get_cookie(req)
  cookie_jar(req)[@key]
end

def cookie_jar(request)
  request.cookie_jar.signed_or_encrypted
end
```

Listing 10-2: Ruby on Rails code that stores session data as a client-side cookie

By using client-side sessions, a site's web servers no longer have to share state. Each web server has everything it needs to reestablish the session with an incoming HTTP request. This is a great bonus when you're trying to scale to thousands of simultaneous users!

Client-side sessions do create an obvious security problem, however. With a naive implementation of client-side sessions, a malicious user can easily manipulate the contents of a session cookie or even forge them entirely. This means the web server has to encode the session state in a way that prevents meddling.

One popular way to secure client-side session cookies is to encrypt the serialized cookie before sending it to the client. The web server then decrypts the cookie when the browser returns it. This approach makes the session state entirely opaque on the client side. Any attempt to manipulate or forge the cookie will corrupt the encoded session and make the cookie unreadable. The server will simply log out the malicious user and redirect them to an error page.

Another, slightly more lightweight approach to securing session cookies is to add a digital signature to the cookie as it's sent. A *digital signature* acts as a unique "fingerprint" for some input data—in this case, the serialized session state—that anyone can easily recalculate as long as they have the signing key originally used to generate the signature. Digitally signing cookies allows the web server to detect attempts to manipulate the session state, since it'll calculate a different signature value and reject the session if there has been any tampering.

Signing cookies rather than encrypting them still allows a nosy user to read the session data in a browser debugger. Bear this in mind if you're storing data about a user—like tracking information—that you might not want them to see!

How Attackers Hijack Sessions

Now that we've discussed sessions and how websites implement them, let's look at how attackers hijack sessions. Attackers use three main methods to hijack sessions: cookie theft, session fixation, and taking advantage of weak session IDs.

Cookie Theft

With the use of cookies being so widespread nowadays, attackers normally achieve session hijacking by stealing the value of a Cookie header from an authenticated user. Attackers usually steal cookies by using one of three techniques: injecting malicious JavaScript into a site as the user interacts with it (cross-site scripting), sniffing network traffic in order to intercept HTTP headers (a man-in-the-middle attack), or triggering unintended HTTP requests to the site when they've already authenticated (cross-site request forgery).

Fortunately, modern browsers implement simple security measures that allow you to protect your session cookies against all three of these techniques. You can enable these security measures simply by adding keywords to the Set-Cookie header returned by the server, as shown in Listing 10-3.

```
Set-Cookie: session_id=2782839109773811992837; HttpOnly; Secure; SameSite=Lax
```

Listing 10-3: A session cookie appearing in an HTTP response that is protected from session hijacking by a combination of keyword instructions

Let's review the three techniques of cookie theft, as well as the keywords that can mitigate them.

Cross-Site Scripting

Attackers often use *cross-site scripting* (which we discussed in detail in Chapter 7) to steal session cookies. An attacker will try to use JavaScript injected into a user's browser to read the user's cookies and send them to an external web server that the attacker controls. The attacker will then *harvest* these cookies as they appear in the web server's log file, and then cut and paste the cookie values into a browser session—or more likely, add them to a script—to perform actions under the hacked user's session.

To defuse session hijacking via cross-site scripting, mark all cookies as HttpOnly in the Set-Cookie header. This tells the browser not to make cookies available to JavaScript code. Append the HttpOnly keyword to the Set-Cookie response header, as shown in Listing 10-4.

```
Set-Cookie: session_id=278283910977381992837; HttpOnly
```

Listing 10-4: Mark your cookies as HttpOnly to stop JavaScript from accessing them.

There's rarely a good reason to allow client-side JavaScript access to cookies, so there are very few downsides to this approach.

Man-in-the-Middle Attacks

An attacker can also steal cookies by using a *man-in-the-middle attack*: the attacker finds a way to sit between the browser and the web server and read network traffic as it passes back and forth. To protect against cookie theft via man-in-the-middle attacks, your website should use HTTPS. You'll learn how to enable HTTPS in Chapter 13.

After you've enabled HTTPS on the web server, you should mark your cookies as Secure, as shown in Listing 10-5, so the browser knows to never send unencrypted cookies over HTTP.

```
Set-Cookie: session_id=278283910977381992837; Secure
```

Listing 10-5: Marking your cookies as secure means adding the Secure keyword to the Set-Cookie response header.

Most web servers are configured to respond to both HTTP and HTTPS, but will redirect HTTP URLs to the HTTPS equivalent. Marking your cookies as Secure will keep the browser from transmitting the cookie data until the redirect has occurred.

Cross-Site Request Forgery

The final way an attacker can hijack sessions is via *cross-site request forgery* (detailed in Chapter 8). An attacker using CSRF doesn't need to get access to a user's session cookie. Instead, they simply need to trick the victim into clicking a link to your site. If the user already has a session open on your site, the browser will send their session cookie along with the HTTP request triggered by the link, which might result in the user inadvertently performing a sensitive action (such as Liking an item the hacker is attempting to promote).

To defuse CSRF attacks, mark your cookies with the SameSite attribute, which instructs the browser to send only session cookies with HTTP requests generated from *your* site. The browser will strip session cookies from other HTTP requests, like those generated by clicking a link in an email.

The SameSite attribute has two settings: Strict and Lax. The Strict setting, shown in Listing 10-6, has the advantage of stripping cookies from all HTTP requests triggered from external sites.

```
Set-Cookie: session_id=278283910977381992837; SameSite=Strict
```

Listing 10-6: The Strict setting will strip cookies from requests generated to your site from external sites.

The `Strict` setting can prove annoying if a user shares your content via social media, because the setting forces anyone clicking their link to log in again to view the content. To solve this annoyance for your users, configure the browser to allow cookies only on `GET` requests by using the `SameSite=Lax` setting, as shown in Listing 10-7.

```
Set-Cookie: session_id=278283910977381992837; SameSite=Lax
```

Listing 10-7: The Lax setting allows for painless sharing of links on social media, while still defusing session-hijacking attacks via CSRF.

This `SameSite=Lax` setting instructs the browser to attach cookies to inbound `GET` requests, while stripping them from other request types. Because websites usually perform sensitive actions (such as writing content or sending messages) through `POST`, `PUT`, or `DELETE` requests, an attacker can't trick a victim into performing these types of sensitive actions.

Session Fixation

In the early history of the internet, many browsers didn't implement cookies, so web servers found other ways to pass session IDs. The most popular way of doing this was by *URL rewriting*—appending the session ID to each URL the user visited. To this day, the *Java Servlet Specification* describes how developers can add session IDs to the end of the URL when cookies aren't available. Listing 10-8 shows an example of a URL rewritten to include a session ID.

```
http://www.example.com/catalog/index.html;jsessionid=1234
```

Listing 10-8: An example of a URL passing the session ID 1234

All browsers have cookie support nowadays, so URL rewriting is an anachronism. However, legacy web stacks may be configured to still accept session IDs in this way, which introduces a couple of major security issues.

First, writing session IDs in the URL allows them to be leaked in log files. An attacker who gets access to your logs can hijack your users' sessions simply by dropping these types of URLs in the browser.

The second issue is a vulnerability called *session fixation*. When web servers vulnerable to session fixation encounter an unknown session ID in a URL, they'll ask the user to authenticate themselves, and then establish a session under the supplied session ID.

This allows a hacker to *fixate* the session ID ahead of time, sending victims tempting links (usually in unsolicited email or spam in a site's comment sections) with the fixated session ID. Any user who clicks the link can have their session hijacked, because the attacker can simply use that same URL in their own browser, having fixed the session ID ahead of time. The act of clicking the link and logging it transforms the dummy session ID into a real session ID—one that the hacker knows.

If your web server supports URL rewriting as a means of session tracking, you should disable it with the relevant configuration options. It serves no purpose and exposes you to session fixation attacks. Listing 10-9 shows how to disable URL rewriting in version 7.0 of the popular Java web server Apache Tomcat by editing the *web.xml* config file.

```
<session-config>
    <tracking-mode>COOKIE</tracking-mode>
</session-config>
```

Listing 10-9: Specifying the session tracking to use the COOKIE mode in Apache Tomcat 7.0 will disable URL rewriting.

Taking Advantage of Weak Session IDs

As we've already discussed, if an attacker gets access to a session ID, they can hijack a user's session. They can do this by stealing a session cookie or by fixating a session ahead of time for servers that support URL rewriting. However, a more brute-force method is to simply *guess* the session ID. Because session IDs are typically just numbers, if these numbers are sufficiently small or predictable, an attacker can write a script to enumerate potential session IDs and test them against the web server until they find a valid session.

Genuinely random numbers are hard to generate in software. Most random number generation algorithms use environmental factors (such as the system's clock time) as *seeds* to generate their random numbers. If an attacker can determine enough of the seed values (or reduce them to a reasonable number of potential values), they can enumerate potentially valid session IDs and test them against your server.

Early versions of the standard Apache Tomcat server were found to be vulnerable to this type of attack. Security researchers discovered that the seeds of the random session ID generation algorithm were the system time and the hashcode of an in-memory object. The researchers were able to use these seeds to narrow the potential input values in such a way that they could reliably guess session IDs.

Consult your web server's documentation and ensure that it uses large session IDs that can't be guessed, generated by a strong random number generation algorithm. Because security researchers frequently discover weak session ID algorithms before attackers can exploit them, make sure to also stay on top of security advisories, which will tell you when you need to patch vulnerabilities in your web stack.

Summary

When a website successfully authenticates a user, the browser and the server open a session between them. Session state can be stored on the server side, or stored on the client side as an encrypted or digitally signed cookie.

Hackers will attempt to steal your session cookies, so you should ensure they're protected. To protect against session hijacking via cross-site scripting, make sure your cookies aren't accessible to JavaScript code. To protect against session hijacking via man-in-the-middle attacks, make sure your cookies are passed only over HTTPS connections. To protect against session hijacking via cross-site request forgery, make sure to strip sensitive cross-site requests of cookies. You can add these protections by using the keywords `HttpOnly`, `SecureOnly`, and `SameSite`, respectively, when you write out your `Set -Cookie` header in the HTTP response.

Older web servers may be vulnerable to session-fixation attacks, so be sure to disable URL rewriting as a way of passing session IDs. Occasionally, web servers are found to use guessable session IDs, so stay aware of security advisories for your software stack and patch it as required.

In the next chapter, you will look at how to correctly implement access control, so malicious users can't access your content or perform actions they aren't supposed to.

11

PERMISSIONS

Users on your website will usually have different levels of permissions. In a content management system, for instance, some users are administrators who have the ability to edit the site's content, while most users can only view and interact with the content. Social media sites have a more complex web of permissions: users may opt to share only certain content with friends or to keep their profile locked. For webmail sites, each user should be able to access only their own email! It's important that you correctly and uniformly enforce these types of permissions across your site, or your users will lose trust in you.

Facebook suffered a disastrous failure in user permissions in September 2018, when hackers exploited a bug in its video uploading tool to generate access tokens for the site. Up to 50 million user accounts on the site were compromised. Hackers stole private profile details like users' names, emails, and phone numbers. Facebook patched the bug, issued a security advisory, and did an apology tour via the press. However, this came at the end of a year that contained a lot of unfavorable stories about Facebook's business practices, and the company's share price took a battering.

The Facebook hack was an example of *privilege escalation*, whereby a malicious user usurps the permissions of another user. The process of securing your site so the correct privileges are applied to each user is called implementing *access control*. This chapter covers both concepts and presents one common method hackers use to exploit insufficient access control, called *directory traversal*.

Privilege Escalation

Security experts divide privilege escalation attacks into two categories: vertical and horizontal escalation.

In *vertical escalation*, an attacker gets access to an account with broader permissions than their own. If an attacker can deploy a *web shell* on your server—an executable script that takes elements of the HTTP request and runs them on the command line—one of their first aims will be to escalate their way to *root privilege*, so they can perform any actions they wish on the server. Ordinarily, commands sent to the web shell will be executed under the same operating system account that the web server is running, which generally has limited network and disk access. Hackers have found a lot of ways to perform vertical escalation attacks on operating systems in an attempt to get root access—which allows them to infect the whole server from a web shell.

In *horizontal escalation*, an attacker accesses another account with similar privileges as their own. In the last couple of chapters, we've discussed common ways of performing this type of attack: guessing passwords, hijacking sessions, or maliciously crafting HTTP request data. The September 2018 Facebook hack was an example of horizontal escalation, caused by an API that issued access tokens without correctly verifying the user's permissions.

To secure your site from escalation attacks, you need to securely implement access control for all sensitive resources. Let's discuss how.

Access Control

Your access control strategy should cover three key aspects:

Authentication   Correctly identifying a user when they return to the site

Authorization   Deciding which actions a user should and shouldn't be able to perform after they've identified themselves

Permission checking   Evaluating authorization at the point in time when a user attempts to perform an action

Chapters 9 and 10 covered authentication in detail; you saw how securing login functionality and session management allows you to reliably determine which user is making HTTP requests. However, from there, you still need to determine which actions each user can perform, and this is a more open-ended problem.

A good access control strategy consists of three stages: designing an authorization model, implementing the access control, and testing the access control. After you've done that, you can also add audit trails and make sure you haven't missed common oversights. Let's go through each of these in detail.

Designing an Authorization Model

There are several common ways to model authorization rules in a software application. When you design your authorization model, it's important to document how you'll apply your chosen model to your users. Without an agreed-upon set of rules, it's hard to define what a "correct" implementation looks like.

With that in mind, let's look at some common ways to model authorization rules.

Access Control Lists

Access control lists (ACLs) are a simple way of modeling authorization that attach against each object in your system a list of permissions, specifying the actions that each user or account can perform on that object. The canonical example of an ACL-based model is the Linux filesystem, which can individually grant each user read, write, or execute permissions on each file and directory. Most SQL databases also implement ACL-based authorization—the account you use to connect to the database determines which tables you can read or update, or whether you can change table structures.

Whitelists and Blacklists

A simpler way to model authorization is to use a whitelist or blacklist. A *whitelist* describes the users or accounts that can access a particular resource, and bans all other users. A *blacklist* explicitly describes the users or accounts that are banned from accessing a resource, implying that the resource should be made accessible to any other user or account. Spam filters frequently use whitelists and blacklists to distinguish email addresses that the email application should send directly to the spam folder or that it should never junk.

Role-Based Access Control

Probably the most comprehensive authorization model is *role-based access control (RBAC)*, which grants users *roles*, or adds users to *groups* that it has granted specific roles. *Policies* in the system define how each role can interact with specific *subjects*—resources within the computing system.

A simple RBAC-system might designate certain users as administrators by adding a user to the Administrators group, which in turn grants them the Administrator role. A policy would then permit users or groups with the Administrator role to edit particular pieces of content of your site.

The Amazon Web Services *identity and access management (IAM)* system is an example of a comprehensive role-based system, as is Microsoft's Active

Directory. Role-based access control is powerful but often prone to complexity. Policies can contradict each other, creating conflicts that developers need to resolve, and users can belong to many groups with overlapping concerns. In such cases, it can sometimes be hard to see why a system is making certain access control decisions, or prioritizing certain rules in a particular set of circumstances.

Ownership-Based Access Control

In the age of social media, it has become common to organize access control rules around the idea of *ownership*, whereby each user has full control over the photos they upload or the posts they create. Social media users are, in essence, administrators of their own content: they can create, upload, delete, and control visibility on their own posts, comments, photos, and stories. They can tag other users in content such as photos, though those other users may have to approve those tags before the tags are made public. On a social media site, each type of content has an implied privacy level: commenting on each other's posts is usually done in public, but direct messages are private (though someone should try explaining that to my grandmother).

Implementing Access Control

After you've chosen your authorization model and defined the access rules for your site, you'll need to implement them in code. You should attempt to centralize access control decisions in your codebase, which makes it easier to validate them against your design documents during code reviews. You don't necessarily need to have all access decisions flow through one code path, but it's important to have a standard method of evaluating access control decisions.

There are many ways of implementing authorization rules: using function or method decorators (which tag functions with certain permission levels), URL checking (for example, prefixing sensitive paths with */admin*), or inserting inline assertions in the code. Some implementations will defer to access control decisions from a dedicated permission component or in-house API. Listing 11-1 shows an example of adding permission checking to Python functions.

```
from django.contrib.auth.decorators import login_required, permission_required

❶ @login_required
❷ @permission_required('content.can_publish')
  def publish_post(request):
      # Publish a post to the front page.
```

Listing 11-1: Checking permissions using the django web server in Python

The web server requires that the user is logged in ❶ and has permissions to publish content ❷ before permitting them to publish a post.

Listing 11-2 shows how to check permissions inline in Ruby, using the pundit library.

```
def publish
  @post = Post.find(params[:id])
❶ authorize @post, :update?
  @post.publish!
  redirect_to @post
end
```

Listing 11-2: Checking permissions by using the pundit *library in Ruby*

The method call ❶ asks the library whether the currently logged-in user has permission to update the social media post described by the @post object.

Whatever method you use to implement permission checking, be sure to make access control decisions based on properly vetted identity data. Don't rely on anything in the HTTP request besides the session cookie to infer which user is accessing a resource and what permissions they have! A malicious user can tamper with anything else in the request in order to commit privilege escalation attacks.

Testing Access Control

It's important to test your access control system critically. Make sure your testing procedures genuinely attempt to find holes in your access control scheme; if you treat it like an attacker would, you'll be better prepared when your first real attack occurs.

Write unit tests that make assertions about who can access certain resources and, more importantly, who *shouldn't* be able to access them. Get in the habit of writing new unit tests describing access control rules as you add features to your site. This is especially important if your site has administrative interfaces, since they're a common backdoor that attackers exploit when hacking websites. Listing 11-3 shows a simple unit test in Ruby that asserts that users must be logged in before performing a sensitive action.

```
class PostsTest < ApplicationSystemTestCase
  test "users should be redirected to the login page if they are not logged in" do
    visit publish_post_url
    assert_response :redirect
    assert_selector "h1", text: "Login"
  end
end
```

Listing 11-3: A Ruby unit test that checks if an unauthorized user is redirected to the login page if they attempt to publish a post

Finally, if you have the time and budget, consider employing an external team to perform penetration testing. The team can probe for missing or erroneous access control rules that an attacker can abuse.

Adding Audit Trails

Because your code will be identifying users and testing their authorization levels as they access resources, you should add audit trails to help with troubleshooting and forensic analysis. *Audit trails* are log files or database entries that are recorded whenever a user performs an action. Simply adding logging statements as users navigate your site (`14:32:06 2019-02-05: User example @gmail.com logged in`) can help you diagnose any problems as they occur at runtime, and provide vital evidence in the event that you do get hacked.

Avoiding Common Oversights

A common oversight you see on many websites is that that they omit access control for resources that aren't designed to be discoverable. It's easy to assume that pages on your site that aren't linked to from elsewhere will be hidden from hackers, because those pages won't be highlighted as hackers crawl your site. This isn't true.

Hacking tools can quickly enumerate private URLs that feature opaque IDs, like *http://example.com/item?id=423242*, and it's even easier to access private URLs with a guessable structure like *http://example.com/profiles/user/bob*. Relying on an attacker being unable to guess a URL is called *security through obscurity* and is considered a risk.

Securing sensitive resources is particularly important for sites designed to *embargo* resources, making them accessible at a certain point in time. Financial reporting sites often operate under this constraint. Publicly traded companies are required to make quarterly or semiannual financial reports available to all investors simultaneously, from previously agreed-upon reporting channels.

Some websites upload these reports early (say, to URLs with the form */reports/<company-name>/<month-year>*), and cheating investors have been known to check these URLs ahead of time in order to access reports before the rest of the market. Financial watchdogs have charged companies large fines for improper disclosure due to broken access logic! Make sure your access control rules account for any timing requirements.

Every sensitive resource on your site requires access control. If your site allows users to download files, hackers may try to access files that they should not be permitted to download, using a hacking method called directory traversal. Let's see how.

Directory Traversal

If any of your website's URLs contain parameters describing paths to files, attackers can use directory traversal to bypass your access control rules. In a *directory traversal* attack, an attacker manipulates the URL parameters in order to access sensitive files that you never intended to be accessible. Directory traversal attacks usually involve replacing a URL parameter with a relative filepath that uses the *../* syntax to "climb out" of the hosting directory. Let's break down how this works.

Filepaths and Relative Filepaths

In most filesystems, the location of each file can be described by a *filepath*. For instance, the filepath */tmp/logs/web.log* on Linux describes the location of the file *web.log* by enumerating the *directories* (in this case, the *logs* directory within the top-level *tmp* directory) that contain the file, joined by a *path separator* character (/).

A *relative filepath* is a filepath that begins with the period (.) character, denoting it as being in the current directory; the relative path *./web.log* describes the location of the file *web.log* as being in the current directory. What's considered the "current" directory depends on the context under which the path is being evaluated. From a command line prompt, for instance, the current directory is the one the user most recently navigated to.

Relative paths also use the .. syntax to reference the containing or *parent* directory. Using the .. syntax twice would reference the parent directory of the parent directory of the current directory. For instance, the filesystem interprets the path *../../etc/passwd* as a request to go up two directories, find a directory called *etc*, and then return the *passwd* file within that directory. Using a relative path is similar to describing a relative: your uncle is your grandparent's son, so to find him, go back two generations in your family tree and then look for a male child.

If your server-side code allows an attacker to pass and evaluate relative filepaths in place of filenames, they can probe your filesystem for interesting-looking files, breaking access control. The relative path syntax lets the attacker read files outside the web server's home directory, letting them probe for directories that commonly hold password or configuration information and read the data contained within them. Let's look at an example of such an attack.

Anatomy of a Directory Traversal Attack

Imagine you have a website that hosts restaurant menus stored as PDFs on your server's filesystem. Your site invites users to download each PDF by clicking a link that references a filename, as shown in Figure 11-1.

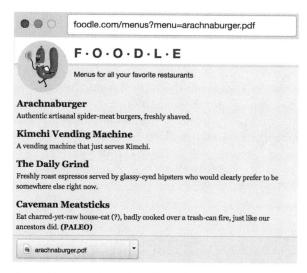

Figure 11-1: A website that allows files to be downloaded

If the filename parameter isn't securely interpreted, an attacker can swap in a relative path in place of the menu filename in the URL, and get access to user account information on your server, as shown in Figure 11-2.

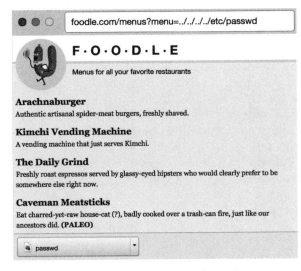

Figure 11-2: Using a directory traversal attack to access a Unix file holding account information

In this instance, the hacker has replaced the name of the menu in the menu parameter with a relative path (../../../../etc/passwd) in order to download a sensitive file. Reading the *passwd* file tells the attacker which user accounts exist on the underlying Linux operating system, revealing sensitive system information that will help the attacker hack the server. You certainly don't want an attacker to be able to read this kind of information! Let's look at ways to defuse directory traversal.

Mitigation 1: Trust Your Web Server

To protect yourself against directory traversal attacks, first familiarize yourself with how your web server resolves static content URLs. Almost all websites will transform URLs into filepaths in some fashion—often when the server answers requests for static content such as JavaScript files, images, or stylesheets. If you find yourself serving more-exotic types of static files (for example, restaurant menus), try to use the web server's built-in URL resolution logic rather than writing your own. Your web server's URL static hosting capabilities are generally battle-tested and secured against directory traversal attacks.

Mitigation 2: Use a Hosting Service

If you serve files that aren't part of your codebase, perhaps because users or site administrators upload them, you should strongly consider hosting them in a content delivery network, in cloud storage, or in a content management system. These software types not only mitigate file upload vulnerabilities, as discussed in Chapter 6, but also defuse directory traversal attacks by allowing you to refer to files either by secure URLs or opaque file identifiers. Of these alternatives, CDNs typically allow for less fine-grained permissions (say, if certain files need to be available to only certain users) but are also typically easiest to integrate with.

Mitigation 3: Use Indirect File References

If you write your own code to serve files from a local disk, the most secure way of defusing directory traversal attacks is via *indirection*: you assign each file an *opaque ID* that corresponds to a filepath, and then have all URLs reference each file by that ID. This requires you to keep some sort of registry that pairs each file ID to a path, say, within a database.

Mitigation 4: Sanitize File References

Finally, if you do end up using direct file references in your URLs—perhaps because you inherit a legacy codebase and lack the time or resources necessary to refactor the way files are stored—you need to secure your site code to ensure that arbitrary paths can't be passed in place of filenames. The most secure approach is simply banning any file reference that includes path separator characters, including *encoded* separator characters. (Note that Windows- and Unix-based operating systems use different path separators: \ and /, respectively.)

Another approach is to validate filenames against a *regular expression (regex)* to filter out anything that looks like path syntax. All modern web programming languages contain some sort of regex implementation, so it's easy to test an incoming filename parameter against a "safe" expression. Be careful with this technique, though: hackers continuously research new and obscure ways to encode pathnames, because directory traversal attacks are so common. If possible, try to use a third-party library to sanitize filenames. Listing 11-4 shows some logic in the Ruby Sinatra gem that sanitizes path parameters.

```
def cleanup(path)
  parts    = []
❶ unescaped = path.gsub(/%2e/i, dot).gsub(/%2f/i, slash).gsub(/%5c/i, backslash)
  unescaped = unescaped.gsub(backslash, slash)

❷ unescaped.split(slash).each do |part|
    next if part.empty? or part == dot
    part == '..' ? parts.pop : parts << part
  end

❸ cleaned = slash + parts.join(slash)
  cleaned << slash if parts.any? and unescaped =~ %r{/\.{0,2}$}
  cleaned
end
```

Listing 11-4: Logic for sanitizing path parameters in the Sinatra Ruby gem

First the code standardizes any obscure character encodings it identifies ❶. Then it splits the path into separate components ❷. Finally, it reconstitutes the path by using a standard separator ❸, ensuring that the leading character is a slash.

The complexity illustrated in Listing 11-4 is necessary because relative paths can be encoded in various ways during a directory traversal attack. Listing 11-5 shows eight ways the parent directory syntax can be encoded on different operating systems.

```
../
..\
..\/
%2e%2e%2f
%252e%252e%252f
%c0%ae%c0%ae%c0%af
%uff0e%uff0e%u2215
%uff0e%uff0e%u2216
```

Listing 11-5: Relative paths can be encoded in many ways for different operating systems. Gulp.

Summary

Users on your website will usually have different levels of permissions, so you need to implement access control rules that are evaluated when a user attempts to access a resource. Access control rules need to be clearly documented, comprehensively implemented, and aggressively tested. Development timelines should include sufficient padding to allow the team to evaluate the security implications of all new code changes.

Static resources that are referred to by filename are vulnerable to directory traversal attacks, a common method of overcoming access control rules. Directory traversal attacks can be thwarted by using your web server's existing method of serving static files, serving static files from a secure third-party system, or referencing static files via indirection. If you're forced to use filenames, make sure to sanitize any HTTP parameters that are used to construct filepaths.

In the next chapter, you'll look at some ways your website may be advertising the technology stack you are using, which will give hackers an idea of how to attack it.

12

INFORMATION LEAKS

Hackers frequently use publicized security vulnerabilities, especially *zero-day vulnerabilities*—security flaws that have been made public in the last 24 hours. When someone publishes a zero-day vulnerability for a software component, hackers will immediately scan for web servers running the vulnerable software in order to exploit the security hole. To protect yourself from such threats, you should ensure that your web server doesn't leak information about the type of software stack you're running on. If you inadvertently advertise your server technology, you're making yourself a target.

In this chapter, you'll learn some common ways web servers leak information about your technology choices and how to mitigate each of these risks.

Mitigation 1: Disable Telltale Server Headers

Make sure to disable any HTTP response headers in your web server configuration that reveal the server technology, language, and version you're running. By default, web servers usually send a Server header back with each response, describing which software is running on the server side. This is great advertising for the web server vendor, but the browser doesn't use it. It simply tells an attacker which vulnerabilities they can probe for. Make sure your web server configuration disables this Server header. (Or if you're feeling mischievous, have it report the wrong web server technology!)

Mitigation 2: Use Clean URLs

When you design your website, avoid telltale file suffixes in URLs, such as *.php*, *.asp*, and *.jsp*. Implement *clean URLs* instead—URLs that do not give away implementation details. URLs with file extensions are common in older web servers, which explicitly reference template filenames. Make sure to avoid such extensions.

Mitigation 3: Use Generic Cookie Parameters

The name of the cookie your web server uses to store session state frequently reveals your server-side technology. For instance, Java web servers usually store the session ID under a cookie named JSESSIONID. Attackers can check these kinds of session cookie names to identify servers, as shown in Listing 12-1.

```
❶ if response.get_cookies.match(/JSESSIONID=(.*);(.*)/i)
    jsessionid = $1
    post_data  = "j_username=#{username}&j_password=#{password}"

    response = send_request_cgi({
                'uri'          => '/admin/j_security_check',
                'method'       => 'POST',
                'content-type' => 'application/x-www-form-urlencoded',
                'cookie'       => "JSESSIONID=#{jsessionid}",
                'data'         => post_data,
            })
```

Listing 12-1: The hacking tool Metasploit attempting to detect and compromise an Apache Tomcat server

Note that the Metasploit code checks the name of the session cookie ❶.

Make sure that your web server sends nothing back in cookies that give clues about your technology stack. Change your configuration to use generic names for the session cookie (for example, session).

Mitigation 4: Disable Client-Side Error Reporting

Most web servers support *client-side error reporting*, which allows the server to print stack traces and routing information in the HTML of the error page. Client-side error reporting is really useful when debugging errors in test environments. However, stack traces and error logs also tell an attacker which modules or libraries you're using, helping them pick out security vulnerabilities to target. Errors occurring in your data access layer can even reveal details about the structure of your database, which is a major security hazard!

You *must* disable error reporting on the client side in your production environment. You should keep the error page your users see completely generic. At most, users should know that an unexpected error occurred and that someone is looking into the problem. Detailed error reports should be kept in production logs and error reporting tools, which only administrators can access.

Consult your web server's documentation on how to disable client-side error reporting. Listing 12-2 illustrates how you would disable this functionality in a Rails config file.

```
# Full error reports are disabled.
config.consider_all_requests_local = false
```

Listing 12-2: Make sure your production configuration file (typically stored at config /environments/production.rb *in Ruby on Rails) disables client-side error reporting.*

Mitigation 5: Minify or Obfuscate Your JavaScript Files

Many web developers preprocess their JavaScript code before deploying it by using a *minifier*, which takes JavaScript code and outputs a functionally equivalent but highly compressed JavaScript file. Minifiers remove all extraneous characters (such as whitespace) and replace some code statements with shorter, semantically identical statements. A related tool is an *obfuscator*, which replaces method and function names with short, meaningless tokens without changing any behavior in the code, deliberately making the code less readable. The popular UglifyJS utility has both capabilities, and can be invoked directly from the command line with the syntax `uglifyjs [input files]`, which makes it straightforward to plug into your build process.

Developers usually minify or obfuscate JavaScript code for performance, because smaller JavaScript files load faster in the browser. This preprocessing also has the positive side effect of making it harder for an attacker to detect which JavaScript libraries you're using. Researchers or attackers periodically discover security vulnerabilities in popular JavaScript libraries that permit cross-site scripting attacks. Making it harder to detect the libraries you're using will give you more breathing room when exploits are discovered.

Mitigation 6: Sanitize Your Client-Side Files

It's important that you conduct code reviews and use static analysis tools to make sure sensitive data doesn't end up in comments or that dead code doesn't get passed to the client. It's easy for developers to leave comments in HTML files, template files, or JavaScript files that share a little too much information, since we forget that these files get shipped to the browser. Minifying JavaScript might strip comments, but you need to spot sensitive comments in template files and hand-coded HTML files during code reviews and remove them.

Hacking tools make it easy for an attacker to crawl your site and extract any comments that you've accidentally left behind—hackers often use this technique to scan for private IP addresses accidentally left in comments. This is often a first port of call when a hacker is attempting to compromise your website.

Stay on Top of Security Advisories

Even with all your security settings locked down, a sophisticated hacker can still make a good guess about the technology you're running. Web servers have telltale behaviors in the way they respond to specific edge cases: deliberately corrupted HTTP requests or requests with unusual HTTP verbs, for example. Hackers can use these unique server-technology fingerprints to identify the server-side technology stack. Even when you follow best practices regarding information leakage, it's important to stay on top of security advisories for the technology you use and deploy patches in a prompt manner.

Summary

You should ensure that your web server doesn't leak information about the type of software stack you're running on, because hackers will use this information against you when trying to figure out how to compromise your website. Make sure your configuration disables telltale headers and uses a generic session cookie name in the HTTP response. Use clean URLs that don't contain filename extensions. Minify or obfuscate your JavaScript so it's harder to tell which third-party libraries you're using. Turn off verbose client-side error reporting in your production site. Make sure to sanitize your template files and HTML for comments that give out too much information. Finally, stay on top of security advisories so you can deploy patches in a timely manner.

In the next chapter, you will take a look at how to secure traffic to your website by using encryption.

13

ENCRYPTION

Encryption powers the modern internet. Without the ability to exchange data packets privately and securely, e-commerce would not exist, and users wouldn't be able to safely authenticate themselves to internet sites.

The HyperText Transfer Protocol Secure is the most widely used form of encryption on the web. Web servers and web browsers universally support HTTPS, so the developer can divert all traffic to that protocol and guarantee secure communication for their users. A web developer who wants to use HTTPS on their site needs only to obtain a *certificate* from a *certificate authority* and install it with their hosting provider.

The ease with which you can get started using encryption belies the complexity of what is happening when a website and user agent interact over HTTPS. Modern *cryptography*—the study of methods of encrypting and decrypting data—depends on techniques developed and actively researched by mathematicians and security professionals. Thankfully, the abstracted layers of the Internet Protocol mean you don't need to know linear algebra or number theory to use their discoveries. But the more you understand about the underlying algorithms, the more you will be able to preempt potential risks.

This chapter first gives a general overview of how encryption is used in the Internet Protocol and the mathematics that underpin it. Once you have a good grasp of how encryption works, you will review the practical steps a developer needs to undertake to get started using HTTPS. Finally, you will look at how hackers take advantage of unencrypted or weakly encrypted traffic, and how some attacks can circumvent encryption entirely.

Encryption in the Internet Protocol

Recall that messages sent over the internet are split into data packets and directed toward their eventual destination via the *Transmission Control Protocol (TCP)*. The recipient computer assembles these TCP packets back into the original message. TCP doesn't dictate *how* the data being sent is meant to be interpreted. For that to happen, both computers need to agree on how to interpret the data being sent, using a higher-level protocol such as HTTP. TCP also does nothing to disguise the content of the packets being sent. Unsecured TCP conversations are vulnerable to *man-in-the-middle attacks*, whereby malicious third parties intercept and read the packets as they are transmitted.

To avoid this, HTTP conversations between a browser and a web server are secured by *Transport Layer Security (TLS)*, a method of encryption that provides both privacy (by ensuring data packets can't be deciphered by a third party) and *data integrity* (by ensuring that any attempt to tamper with the packets in transit will be detectable). HTTP conversations conducted using TLS are called *HTTP Secure (HTTPS)* conversations.

When your web browser connects to an HTTPS website, the browser and web server negotiate which encryption algorithms to use as part of the *TLS handshake*—the exchange of data packets that occurs when a TLS conversation is initiated. To make sense of what happens during the TLS handshake, we need to take a brief detour into the various types of encryption algorithms. Time for some light mathematics!

Encryption Algorithms, Hashing, and Message Authentication Codes

An *encryption algorithm* takes input data and scrambles it by using an *encryption key*—a secret shared between two parties wishing to initiate secure communication. The scrambled output is indecipherable to anyone without a *decryption key*—the corresponding key required to unscramble the data. The input data and keys are typically encoded as binary data, though the keys may be expressed as strings of text for readability.

Many encryption algorithms exist, and more continue to be invented by mathematicians and security researchers. They can be classified into a few categories: symmetric and asymmetric encryption algorithms (for ciphering data), hash functions (for fingerprinting data and building other cryptographic algorithms), and message authentication codes (for ensuring data integrity).

Symmetric Encryption Algorithms

A *symmetric encryption algorithm* uses the same key to encrypt and decrypt data. Symmetric encryption algorithms usually operate as *block ciphers*: they break the input data into fixed-size blocks that can be individually encrypted. (If the last block of input data is undersized, it will be *padded* to fill out the block size.) This makes them suitable for processing streams of data, including TCP data packets.

Symmetric algorithms are designed for speed but have one major security flaw: the decryption key must be given to the receiving party before they decrypt the data stream. If the decryption key is shared over the internet, potential attackers will have an opportunity to steal the key, which allows them to decrypt any further messages. Not good.

Asymmetric Encryption Algorithms

In response to the threat of decryption keys being stolen, *asymmetric encryption algorithms* were developed. Asymmetric algorithms use different keys to encrypt and decrypt data.

An asymmetric algorithm allows a piece of software such as a web server to publish its encryption key freely, while keeping its decryption key a secret. Any user agent looking to send secure messages to the server can encrypt those messages by using the server's encryption key, secure in the knowledge that nobody (not even themselves!) will be able to decipher the data being sent, because the decryption key is kept secret. This is sometimes described as *public-key cryptography*: the encryption key (*the public key*) can be published; only the decryption key (the *private key*) needs to be kept secret.

Asymmetric algorithms are significantly more complex and hence slower than symmetric algorithms. Encryption in the Internet Protocol uses a combination of both types, as you will see later in the chapter.

Hash Functions

Related to encryption algorithms are *cryptographic hash functions*, which can be thought of as encryption algorithms whose output *cannot* be decrypted. Hash functions also have a couple of other interesting properties: the output of the algorithm (the *hashed value*) is always a fixed size, regardless of the size of input data; and the chances of getting the same output value, given different input values, is astronomically small.

Why on earth would you want to encrypt data you couldn't subsequently decrypt? Well, it's a neat way to generate a "fingerprint" for input data. If you need to check that two separate inputs are the same but don't want to store the raw input values for security reasons, you can verify that both inputs produce the same hashed value.

This is how website passwords are typically stored, as we saw in Chapter 9. When a password is first set by a user, the web server will store the hashed value of the password in the database but will deliberately forget the actual password value. When the user later reenters their password on the site, the server will recalculate the hashed value and compare it with the stored hashed value. If the two hashed values differ, it indicates the user entered a different password, which means the credentials should be rejected. In this way, a site can check the correctness of passwords without explicitly knowing each user's password. (Storing passwords in plaintext form is a security hazard: if an attacker compromises the database, they get every user's password.)

Message Authentication Codes

Message authentication code (MAC) algorithms are similar to (and generally built on top of) cryptographic hash functions, in that they map input data of an arbitrary length to a unique, fixed-sized output. This output is itself called a *message authentication code.* MAC algorithms are more specialized than hash functions, however, because recalculating a MAC requires a secret key. This means that only the parties in possession of the secret key can generate or check the validity of message authentication codes.

MAC algorithms are used to ensure that the data packets transmitted on the internet cannot be forged or tampered with by an attacker. To use a MAC algorithm, the sending and receiving computers exchange a shared, secret key—usually as part of the TLS handshake. (The secret key will itself be encrypted before it is sent, to avoid the risk of it being stolen.) From that point onward, the sender will generate a MAC for each data packet being sent and attach the MAC to the packet. Because the recipient computer has the same key, it can recalculate the MAC from the message. If the calculated MAC differs from the value attached to the packet, this is evidence that the packet has been tampered with or corrupted in some form, or it was not sent by the original computer. Hence, the recipient rejects the data packet.

If you've gotten to this point and are still paying attention, congratulations! Cryptography is a large, complex subject that has its own particular jargon. Understanding how it fits into the Internet Protocol requires balancing multiple concepts in your head at once, so thank you for your patience. Let's see how the various types of cryptographic algorithms we have discussed are used by TLS.

The TLS Handshake

TLS uses a combination of cryptographic algorithms to efficiently and safely pass information. For speed, most data packets passed over TLS will be encrypted using a symmetric encryption algorithm commonly referred to as the *block cipher,* since it encrypts "blocks" of streaming information. Recall that symmetric encryption algorithms are vulnerable to having their encryption keys stolen by malicious users eavesdropping on the conversation. To safely pass the encryption/decryption key for the block cipher, TLS will encrypt the key by using an *asymmetric* algorithm before passing it to the recipient. Finally, data packets passed using TLS will be tagged using a message authentication code, to detect if any data has been tampered with.

At the start of a TLS conversation, the browser and website perform a *TLS handshake* to determine how they should communicate. In the first stage of the handshake, the browser will list multiple cipher suites that it supports. Let's drill down on what this means.

Cipher Suites

A *cipher suite* is a set of algorithms used to secure communication. Under the TLS standard, a cipher suite consists of *three* separate algorithms. The first algorithm, the *key-exchange algorithm*, is an asymmetric encryption algorithm. This is used by communicating computers to exchange secret keys for the second encryption algorithm: the symmetric block cipher designed for encrypting the content of TCP packets. Finally, the cipher suite specifies a MAC algorithm for authenticating the encrypted messages.

Let's make this more concrete. A modern web browser such as Google Chrome that supports TLS 1.3 offers numerous cipher suites. At the time of writing, one of these suites goes by the catchy name of ECDHE-ECDSA-AES128-GCM-SHA256. This particular cipher suite includes ECDHE-RSA as the key-exchange algorithm, AES-128-GCM as the block cipher, and SHA-256 as the message authentication algorithm.

Want some more, entirely unnecessary, detail? Well, *ECDHE* stands for *Elliptic Curve Diffie–Hellman Exchange* (a modern method of establishing a shared secret over an insecure channel). *RSA* stands for the *Rivest–Shamir–Adleman* algorithm (the first practical asymmetric encryption algorithm, invented by three mathematicians in the 1970s after drinking a lot of Passover wine). *AES* stands for the *Advanced Encryption Standard* (an algorithm invented by two Belgian cryptographers and selected by the National Institute of Standards and Technology through a three-year review process). This particular variant uses a 128-bit key in Galois/Counter Mode, which is specified by *GCM* in the name. Finally, SHA-256 stands for the *Secure Hash Algorithm* (a hash function with a 256-bit word size).

See what I mean about the complexity of modern encryption standards? Modern browsers and web servers support a fair number of cipher suites, and more get added to the TLS standard all the time. As weaknesses are discovered in existing algorithms, and computing power gets cheaper, security researchers update the TLS standard to keep the internet secure. As a web developer, it's not particularly important to understand how these algorithms work, but it *is* important to keep your web server software up-to-date so you can support the most modern, secure algorithms.

Session Initiation

Let's continue where we left off. In the second stage of the TLS handshake, the web server selects the most secure cipher suite it can support and then instructs the browser to use those algorithms for communication. At the same time, the server passes back a *digital certificate*, containing the server name, the trusted certificate authority that will vouch for the authenticity of the certificate, and the web server's encryption key to be used in the key-exchange algorithm. (We will discuss what certificates are and why they are necessary for secure communication in the next section.)

Once the browser verifies the authenticity of the certificate, the two computers generate a *session key* that will be used to encrypt the TLS conversation with the chosen block cipher. (Note that this session key is different from the HTTP *session identifier* discussed in previous chapters. TLS handshakes occur at a lower level of the Internet Protocol than the HTTP conversation, which has not begun yet.) The session key is a large random number generated by the browser, encrypted with the (public) encryption key attached to the digital certificate using the key-exchange algorithm, and transmitted to the server.

Now, finally, the TLS conversation can begin. Everything past this point will be securely encrypted using the block cipher and the shared session identifier, so the data packets will be indecipherable to anyone snooping on the conversation. The browser and server use the agreed-upon encryption algorithm and session key to encrypt packets in both directions. Data packets are also authenticated and tamper-proof, using message authentication codes.

As you can see, a lot of complex mathematics underpin secure communication on the internet. Thankfully, the steps involved for enabling HTTPS as a web developer are much simpler. Now we have the theory out of the way, let's take a look at the practical steps needed to secure your users.

Enabling HTTPS

Securing traffic for your website is a lot easier than understanding the underlying encryption algorithms. Most modern web browsers are self-updating; the development teams for each major browser will be on the cutting edge of supporting modern TLS standards. The latest version of your web server software will support similarly modern TLS algorithms. That means that the only responsibility left to you as a developer is to obtain a digital certificate and install it on your web server. Let's discuss how to do that and illuminate why certificates are necessary.

Digital Certificates

A *digital certificate* (also known as a *public-key certificate*) is an electronic document used to prove ownership of a public encryption key. Digital certificates are used in TLS to associate encryption keys with internet domains (such as *example.com*). They are issued by *certificate authorities*, which act as a trusted third party between a browser and a website, vouching that a given encryption key should be used to encrypt data being sent to the website's domain. Browser software will trust a few hundred certificate authorities— for example, Comodo, DigiCert, and, more recently, the nonprofit Let's Encrypt. When a trusted certificate authority vouches for a key and domain, it assures your browser that it's communicating with the right website using the right encryption key, thereby blocking an attacker from presenting a malicious website or certificate.

You might ask: why is a third party required to exchange encryption keys on the internet? After all, isn't the whole point of asymmetric encryption that the public key can be made available freely by the server itself? While this statement is true, the actual process of fetching an encryption key on the internet depends on the reliability of the internet's *Domain Name System (DNS)* that maps domain names to IP addresses. Under some circumstances, DNS is vulnerable to *spoofing attacks* that can be used to direct internet traffic away from a legitimate server to an IP address controlled by an attacker. If an attacker can spoof an internet domain, they can issue their own encryption key, and victims would be none the wiser.

Certificate authorities exist to prevent encrypted traffic from being spoofed. Should an attacker find a way to divert traffic from a legitimate (secure) website to a malicious server under their control, that attacker will typically not possess the decryption key corresponding to the website's certificate. This means they will be unable to decrypt intercepted traffic that was encrypted using the encryption key attached to the site's digital certificate.

On the other hand, if the attacker presents an *alternative* digital certificate corresponding to a decryption key that they *do* possess, that certificate will not have been verified by a trusted certificate authority. Any browser visiting the spoofed website will show a security warning to the user, strongly dissuading them from continuing.

In this way, certificate authorities allow users to trust the websites they are visiting. You can view the certificate a website is using by clicking the padlock icon in the browser bar. The information described there won't be particularly interesting, but browsers do a good job of warning you when a certificate is invalid.

Obtaining a Digital Certificate

Obtaining a digital certificate for your website from a certificate authority requires a few steps, by which the authority verifies that you own your domain. The precise way you perform these steps differs depending on which certificate authority you choose.

The first step is to generate a *key pair*, a small digital file containing randomly generated public and private encryption keys. Next, you use this key pair to generate a *certificate signing request (CSR)* that contains the public key and domain name of your website, and upload the request to a certificate authority. Before honoring the signing request and issuing the certificate, the certificate authority will require you to demonstrate to them that you have control of the internet domain contained in the CSR. Once domain ownership has been verified, you can download the certificate and install it on your web server along with the key pair.

Generating a Key Pair and Certificate Signing Request

The key pair and CSR are typically generated using the command line tool, openssl. CSRs often contain other information about the applicant besides the domain name and public key, such as the organization's legal name and physical location. These get included in the signed certificate, but are not mandatory unless the certificate authority chooses to validate them. During the generation of the signing request, the domain name is often referred to as the *distinguished name (DN)* or the *fully qualified domain name (FQDN)*, for historical reasons. Listing 13-1 shows how to generate a certificate signing request by using openssl.

```
openssl req -new -key ./private.key -out ./request.csr
```

Listing 13-1: Generating a certificate signing request by using openssl on the command line

The file *private.key* should contain a newly generated private key (which can also be generated with openssl). The tool openssl will ask for details to incorporate into the signing request, including the domain name.

Domain Verification

Domain verification is the process by which a certificate authority verifies that someone applying for a certificate for an internet domain does indeed have control of that domain. When applying for a digital certificate, you are stating that you need to be able to decrypt traffic sent to a particular internet domain. The certificate authority will insist on checking that you own that domain as part of its due diligence.

Domain verification generally requires you to make a temporary edit to the DNS entries for your domain, thus demonstrating that you have edit rights in the DNS. Domain verification is what protects against DNS spoofing attacks: an attacker cannot apply for a certificate unless they also have edit rights.

Extended Validation Certificates

Some certificate authorities issue *extended validation (EV)* certificates. These require the certificate authority to collect and verify information about the legal entity applying for a certificate. That information will then be included in the digital certificate, and made available in the web browser to users visiting the website. EV certificates are popular with large organizations, because the name of the company is usually displayed alongside the padlock icon in the browser URL bar, encouraging a sense of trust in users.

Expiring and Revoking Certificates

Digital certificates have a finite lifespan (typically in years or months) after which they must be reissued by the certificate authority. Certificate authorities also keep track of certificates that have been voluntarily *revoked* by certificate holders. If the private key corresponding to your digital certificate gets compromised, it's important that you as a site owner apply for a new certificate and then revoke the prior certificate. Browsers will warn a user when visiting a website with an expired or revoked certificate.

Self-Signed Certificates

For some environments, particularly testing environments, acquiring a certificate from a certificate authority is unnecessary or impractical. Testing environments that are available on only an internal network, for example, can't be verified by a certificate authority. You may still want to support

HTTPS on these environments, however, so the solution is to generate your own certificate—a *self-signed certificate.*

Command line tools like `openssl` can easily produce self-signed certificates. Browsers encountering a site with a self-signed certificate will usually issue a strident security warning to the user (`This site's security certificate is not trusted!`) but will still allow the user to accept the risks and continue anyway. Just make sure anyone using your test environment is aware of this limitation and knows why the warning occurs.

Should You Pay for Certificates?

Certificate authorities were traditionally commercial entities. Even today, many of them charge a fixed fee for each certificate being issued. Since 2015, the California nonprofit Let's Encrypt has offered free certificates. Let's Encrypt was founded by (among others) the Mozilla Foundation (which coordinates releases of the Firefox browser) and the Electronic Frontier Foundation (a digital rights nonprofit based in San Francisco). As a result, there is little reason to pay for a certificate, unless you require extended validation capabilities offered by commercial certificate authorities.

Installing a Digital Certificate

Once you have a certificate and a key pair, the next step is to get your web server to switch to using HTTPS and serve the certificate as part of the TLS handshake. This process varies depending on your hosting provider and server technology, though it's normally pretty straightforward and well-documented. Let's review a typical deployment process—which will require a short digression.

Web Servers vs. Application Servers

Up to this point in the book, I have described web servers as machines for intercepting and answering HTTP requests, and talked about how they either send back static content or execute code in response to each request. While this is an accurate description, it elides the fact that websites are usually deployed as a *pair* of running applications.

The first of the applications that runs a typical website is a *web server* that serves static content and performs low-level TCP functions. This will typically be something like Nginx or the Apache HTTP Server. Web servers are written in C and optimized to quickly perform low-level TCP functions.

The second application of the pair is an *application server,* which sits downstream from the web server and hosts the code and templates that make up that dynamic content of the site. Many application servers are available for each programming language. A typical application server might be Tomcat or Jetty for websites written in the Java languages; Puma or Unicorn for Ruby on Rails websites; Django, Flask, or Tornado for Python websites; and so on.

Rather confusingly, web developers will often casually refer to the application server they use as "the web server," since that is the environment they spent most of the time writing code for. In actual fact, it's perfectly possible to deploy an application server on its own, because an application server can do everything a web server can, albeit less efficiently. This is a fairly typical setup when a web developer is writing and testing code on their own machine.

Configuring Your Web Server to Use HTTPS

Digital certificates and encryption keys are almost always deployed to web servers, since they are much faster than application servers. Switching over a web server to use HTTPS is a matter of updating the web server's configuration so that it accepts traffic on the standard HTTPS port (443), and telling it the location of the digital certificate and key pair to be used when establishing the TLS session. Listing 13-2 shows how to add the certificate into the configuration file for the Nginx web server.

```
server {
    listen              443 ssl;
    server_name         www.example.com;
    ssl_certificate     www.example.com.crt;
    ssl_certificate_key www.example.com.key;
    ssl_protocols       TLSv1.2 TLSv1.3;
    ssl_ciphers         HIGH:!aNULL:!MD5;
}
```

Listing 13-2: Describing the location of the digital certificate (www.example.com.crt) and encryption key (www.example.com.key) when configuring Nginx

Web servers that handle TLS functionality in this way will decrypt incoming HTTPS requests, and pass any requests that need to be handled by the application server downstream as unencrypted HTTP requests. This is called *terminating HTTPS* at the web server: traffic between the web and application server is not secure (because the encryption has been stripped), but this isn't usually a security risk because traffic is not leaving the physical machine (or at least, will only be passed over a private network).

What About HTTP?

Configuring your web server to listen for HTTPS requests on port 443 requires a handful of edits to a configuration file. You then need to decide how your web server will treat unencrypted traffic on the standard HTTP port (80). The usual method is to instruct the web server to redirect insecure traffic to the corresponding secure URL. For instance: if a user agent visits *http://www.example.com/page/123*, the web server will respond with an HTTP 301 response, directing the user agent to visit *https://www.example .com/page/123* instead. The browser will understand this as an instruction to send the same request on port 443, after negotiating a TLS handshake. Listing 13-3 shows an example of how to redirect all traffic on port 80 to port 443 on the Nginx web server.

```
server {
    listen 80 default_server;
    server_name _;
    return 301 https://$host$request_uri;
}
```

Listing 13-3: Redirecting all HTTP to HTTPS on the Nginx web server

HTTP Strict Transport Security

At this point, your site is set up to securely communicate with the browser, and any browsers using HTTP will get redirected to HTTPS. You have one final loophole to take care of: you need to ensure that sensitive data will not be sent during any initial connection over HTTP.

When a browser visits a site it has seen previously, the browser sends back any cookies the website previously supplied in the Cookie header of a request. If the initial connection to the website is done over HTTP, that cookie information will be passed insecurely, even if the subsequent requests and responses get upgraded to HTTPS.

Your website should instruct browsers to send cookies *only* over an HTTPS connection by implementing an *HTTP Strict Transport Security (HSTS)* policy. You do this by setting the header Strict-Transport-Security in your responses. A modern browser encountering this header will remember to connect to your site *only* using HTTPS. Even if the user explicitly types in an HTTP address like *http://www.example.com*, the browser will switch to using HTTPS without being prompted. This protects cookies from being stolen during the initial connection to your site. Listing 13-4 shows how to add a Strict-Transport-Security header when using Nginx.

```
server {
    add_header Strict-Transport-Security "max-age=31536000" always;
}
```

Listing 13-4: Setting up HTTP Strict Transport Security in Nginx

The browser will remember not to send any cookies over HTTP for the number of seconds supplied in max-age, whereupon it will check again if the site has changed its policy.

Attacking HTTP (and HTTPS)

At this point in the chapter, you might well ask: what's the worst that can happen if I choose *not* to use HTTPS? I haven't really described how unencrypted HTTP can be exploited, so let's remedy that. Weakly encrypted or unencrypted communication on the internet allows an attack to launch a man-in-the-middle attack, whereby they tamper with or snoop on the HTTP conversation. Let's look at some recent examples from hackers, internet service providers, and governments.

Wireless Routers

Wireless routers are a common target for man-in-the-middle attacks. Most routers contain a bare-bones installation of the Linux operating system, which enables them to route traffic to a local *internet service provider (ISP)* and host a simple configuration interface. This is a perfect target for a hacker, because the Linux installation will typically *never* be updated with security patches—and the same operating system version will be installed in many thousands of homes.

In May 2018, Cisco security researchers discovered that over half a million Linksys and Netgear routers had been infected with a piece of malware called *VPNFilter*, which snooped on HTTP traffic passing through the router, stealing website passwords and other sensitive user data on behalf of an unknown attacker thought to be linked to the Russian government. VPNFilter even attempted to perform *downgrade attacks*, interfering with the initial TLS handshake to popular sites so that the browser opted to use weaker encryption or no encryption at all.

Sites using HTTPS would have been immune to this attack, because HTTPS traffic is indecipherable to anyone but the recipient site. Traffic to other websites was likely stolen by hackers and mined for sensitive data.

Wi-Fi Hotspots

A lower-tech way for a hacker to launch a man-in-the-middle attack is to simply set up their own Wi-Fi hotspot in a public place. Few of us pay much attention to the name of the Wi-Fi hotspots our devices use, so it's easy for an attacker to set up a hotspot in a public space like a café or hotel lobby and wait for unwary users to connect to it. Because TCP traffic will flow through the hacker's device on its way to the ISP, the hacker will be able to record the traffic to disk and comb through it to extract sensitive details like credit card numbers and passwords. The only indication to the victim that anything untoward has happened occurs when the attacker leaves the physical location and shuts down the hotspot, disconnecting their victims from the internet. Encrypting traffic defeats this attack, since the hacker will not be able to read any traffic they captured.

Internet Service Providers

Internet service providers connect individual users and businesses to the internet backbone, which is a position of enormous trust given the potentially sensitive nature of the data being passed. You would think that would deter them from snooping or interfering with HTTP requests, but that isn't the case for companies like Comcast, one of the largest ISPs in the United States, which injected JavaScript advertisements into HTTP traffic flowing through its servers for many years. Comcast claimed to be doing this as a service (many of the advertisements informed the user of how much of the monthly data plan had already been used), but digital rights campaigners saw this approach as analogous to a mail carrier slipping advertising material into sealed letters.

Websites that use HTTPS are immune to this type of tampering, because the contents of each request and response are opaque to the ISP.

Government Agencies

Government agencies snooping on your internet traffic might seem like the stuff of conspiracy theories, but plenty of evidence indicates this does indeed happen. The US *National Security Agency (NSA)* has successfully implemented man-in-middle-attacks to conduct surveillance. An internal presentation leaked by former NSA contractor Edward Snowden described how Brazil's state-run oil producer Petrobras was spied on: the NSA obtained digital certificates for Google websites and then hosted its own look-alike sites that harvested user credentials while proxying traffic to Google. We don't really know how widespread this type of program is, but it's pretty unnerving to think about. (In case anyone from the government is reading this: actually, this type of program is good and keeps us safe, and the author of this book supports it wholeheartedly.)

Summary

You should use HTTPS to ensure that communication from web browsers to your site is kept private and cannot be tampered with. HTTPS is HTTP sent over Transport Layer Security (TLS). A TLS conversation is initiated when a web server and user agent partake in a TLS handshake. During the TLS handshake, the browser offers a list of supported cipher suites it is able to support. Each cipher suite contains a key-exchange algorithm, a block cipher, and a message authentication code algorithm. The web server picks a cipher it supports and returns its digital certificate.

The browser then uses the public key attached to the digital certificate to encrypt a (randomly generated) TLS session identifier with the key-exchange algorithm, and sends it to the web server. Finally, when both parties possess the session identifier, they use it as the encryption/decryption key for subsequent messages sent back and forth, encrypted with the chosen block cipher. The authenticity of each data packet will be validated using the message authentication code algorithm.

Digital certificates are issued by a handful of certificate authorities, which will require you to demonstrate ownership of your chosen domain in the Domain Name System before issuing a certificate. By acting as a trusted third party between the browser and the website, certificate authorities prevent spoofed websites from presenting a fake certificate.

Once you have obtained a certificate for your website, you need to serve content over HTTPS. This means configuring your web server to accept traffic over port 443, telling it where to find the certificate and corresponding decryption key, and redirecting HTTP traffic on port 80 to HTTPS traffic on port 443. Finally, you should instruct the browser not to send any sensitive data—for example, session cookies—in HTTP requests before the upgrade to HTTPS, by setting an HTTP Strict Transport Security policy.

Be sure to upgrade your web server technology fairly frequently, so you are certain you are using the most modern (and hence secure) cipher suites. Encryption standards are constantly being researched and enhanced, as older algorithms are compromised or discovered to be vulnerable.

While we are discussing the need to keep your web server up-to-date, you should take a broader look at how to test, secure, and manage any third-party applications you use to serve your website. That's exactly what you will be doing in the next chapter!

14

THIRD-PARTY CODE

Nobody builds software from scratch nowadays, least of all web developers. Most of the code powering your website—from the operating system, to the web server, to the programming language libraries you use—will be written by others. So how do you manage vulnerabilities in other people's code?

Hackers often target known vulnerabilities in popular software components, so it is important to secure third-party code. It is far more efficient for a hacker to scan the web for insecure WordPress instances, for example, than to pick a particular website and try to figure out how it might be vulnerable. So, it's important that you stay up-to-date with the latest security patches in order to avoid being picked up by a malicious scan.

This chapter discusses three approaches to securing third-party code. You'll learn how to stay ahead of security advisories for your *dependencies*, the software components you use. Next, you'll delve into the importance of *configuring* these dependencies correctly, so they do not accidentally leave open backdoors that hackers can take advantage of. Finally, you'll see the security risks associated with third-party *services*—code running on other people's servers that is either called by your web server or loaded into your web pages via JavaScript imports. In particular, you will look at the alarmingly popular strategy of deploying malware through ad networks—so-called *malvertising*—and examine ways to protect your users if your site includes advertising.

Securing Dependencies

In April 2014, the authors of OpenSSL, the open source C library that implements TLS for most versions of Linux (and other operating systems), disclosed the existence of the Heartbleed bug: using a buffer over-read, an attacker could read arbitrary chunks of memory from a server using the vulnerable library, and thereby steal encryption keys, usernames, passwords, and other sensitive data. The two most popular web servers on the internet—Apache and Nginx—use OpenSSL to secure communication, and researchers working for the security firm AVG estimated that more than half a million websites were revealed to be vulnerable to attack overnight. Because of the sheer number of websites affected, the Heartbleed vulnerability has been called the most dangerous bug of all time.

A new version of OpenSSL that patched the bug was released the same day that the vulnerability was disclosed, but unpatched web servers were still common on the internet for months afterward. This was a dangerous time to run an unpatched web server: hackers had time to find the best methods of exploiting the vulnerability, and the dwindling pool of vulnerable sites made the remaining web servers a more likely target.

All websites use third-party code, and all third-party libraries—even those written by security experts, like OpenSSL—are liable to have security issues. If you want to stay ahead of these vulnerabilities, you need to be aware of security issues as soon as they are made public and to patch software promptly. There are three aspects to this: knowing precisely what dependencies you are running, being able to update your dependencies quickly, and staying alert to security issues for your dependencies. Let's discuss each in turn.

Know What Code You Are Running

The first step to securing your dependencies is knowing what they are. This might sound obvious, but modern software stacks are intricate and multilayered, making it easy to add new libraries during the development phase of the software development life cycle that you may forget about later. There are numerous tools you really ought to be using to organize your dependencies.

Dependency Management Tools

Most programming languages come with a *dependency manager* that allows a development team to specify third-party dependencies in a configuration file. The described software libraries will be downloaded on demand as part of the build process. Dependency managers make it easy to grab new dependencies and to rebuild the software stack in a new environment—for instance, when you deploy to a server.

To be absolutely sure you know which versions of each dependency you are running, you should get in the habit of specifying explicit *version numbers* for each dependency in your dependency list. Packages available in a dependency management system are hosted in a remote repository on the internet. As package authors release new versions of a package, they will be added to the repository with a new version number. By default, most dependency managers grab the latest version of each dependency when you first run a build in a new environment. This is a sensible default behavior during initial development, but by the time you are releasing code, your dependency configuration file should explicitly list version numbers. Security advisories will disclose which versions of a dependency are vulnerable, so pinning down the versions you are running in each environment will tell you what needs to be patched.

Be aware, too, that the dependencies you declare likely have dependencies themselves—and your dependency manager will helpfully fetch those libraries too. For this reason, we talk about the *dependency tree*, since each dependency has branches that are other dependencies. Be sure to consider the *whole* dependency tree when assessing security risks. Your dependency manager will be able to output the whole tree (including dependencies of dependencies) on the command line. Listing 14-1 shows the dependency tree for a Node.js project, illustrating how the @blueprintjs/core library has the popper.js library as a subdependency.

```
my_project@0.0.0 /usr/code/my_project
├─┬ @blueprintjs/core@3.10.0
│ ├─┬ @blueprintjs/icons@3.4.0
│ │ ├── classnames@2.2.6 deduped
│ │ └── tslib@1.9.3 deduped
│ ├── @types/dom4@2.0.1
│ ├── classnames@2.2.6 deduped
│ ├── dom4@2.1.4
│ ├── normalize.css@8.0.1
│ ├── popper.js@1.14.6
│ ├── react-popper@1.3.3 deduped
```

Listing 14-1: The command npm list shows the whole dependency tree in the Node Package Manager.

Operating System Patches

In addition to tracking your programming language dependencies, you also need to keep track of software packages deployed at the operating system level. Operating system vendors (for example, Red Hat and Microsoft) frequently issue security patches, so you should track the version of each operating system library you are using in any given environment, and have a strategy for upgrading servers in a timely fashion. If you have physical servers running in a data center, your company likely has dedicated system administrators to take care of this. If you run your software on virtualized servers in the cloud (for instance, on Amazon EC2), you should update the version of the operating system regularly as part of deployment. Using Docker for containerization is a great way of tracking operating system dependencies, too, since the Docker configuration file will explicitly list what software is to be installed when the container is instantiated.

Integrity Checks

One final consideration: you need to ensure that the code you *think* you are running is the code you are *actually* running. Dependency managers and patching tools will help here. They ensure that software components are delivered uncorrupted by using *checksums*—digital fingerprints that are calculated when the dependency is uploaded to the repository, and that can be recalculated and verified when the dependency is downloaded for use. You should strive to provide the same guarantees when deploying JavaScript code and other resources to the browser.

Modern browsers allow you to do this by adding *subresource integrity checks* to <script> and <style> tags in your HTML. Your build process should generate a checksum for each resource file you intend to import on the client side, and assign that checksum to the integrity attribute of each import tag. Listing 14-2 shows how to use the openssl utility to generate a checksum.

```
cat FILENAME.js | openssl dgst -sha384 -binary | openssl base64 -A
```

Listing 14-2: To generate a checksum in Unix, pipe the JavaScript file FILENAME.js to openssl to generate a digest and encode it in Base64.

The browser will compare the script to the expected checksum and verify that there's a match before executing the imported code. This makes it much harder for hackers who gain access to your server to replace JavaScript files with malicious code, because they would also have to gain access to and change the code that generates the <script> tags, like the one shown in Listing 14-3.

```
<script src="https://example.com/example-framework.js"
        integrity="sha384-oqVuAfXRKap7fdgcCY5uykM6+R9GqQ8K/uxy9rx7HNQlG"
        crossorigin="anonymous"></script>
```

Listing 14-3: Ensure the integrity of an imported JavaScript file by calculating a checksum of the file and adding it to the integrity attribute of the HTML tag that imports the script.

Be Able to Deploy New Versions Quickly

Responding to security issues requires you to be able to deploy patches quickly, which means, in turn, having an orderly and scripted release process. Chapter 5 covered much of this: your release process should be reliable, reproducible, and revertible, and releases should be tied to code branches in a source control system. The configuration file used by your dependency manager should be kept under source control, so you can track which versions of each dependency were deployed with each release.

You will often deploy security patches for third-party components in isolation—upgrading *dependency* versions without releasing any changes to your own code. A release that contains only third-party code changes still requires you to *regression test* your website: in other words, to ensure that the upgraded dependencies do not break any existing functionality on the site. Regression testing becomes much more of a formality if you have good coverage in your unit tests. The more lines of your codebase that are executed during unit test runs, the less manual testing you will need to do. Investing some time in writing good unit tests will make deploying security patches quicker and easier.

Stay Alert to Security Issues

With carefully managed dependencies and a reliable release process, you are in a good position to secure the third-party code you use. The final piece of the puzzle is staying in the loop when security issues are disclosed. Thanks to the internet, you have a lot of ways to keep track.

Social Media

Security advisories spread quickly through social media and news sites like Twitter, Reddit, and Hacker News (*https://news.ycombinator.com/*), so these sites are a great way to get security news quickly. Big software vulnerabilities will be discussed in subreddits like *https://www.reddit.com/r/programming/* and */r/technology*, and will usually hit the front page of Hacker News.

If you make time to follow technology pundits and software authors on Twitter, security issues will often be the topic of the day. It's also a great way to keep abreast of new developments in the software world.

Mailing Lists and Blogs

Programming languages often have mailing lists and channels that publish big news. The Python Software Foundation publishes a weekly newsletter and has its own Slack channel, for instance. Make sure to subscribe to anything relevant to your technology stack.

A huge number of blogs exist on the topic of information security. Check out Brian Krebs (*https://krebsonsecurity.com/*) and Bruce Schneier (*https://www.schneier.com/*) for insightful commentary on the security issues of the day.

Official Advisories

Pay attention to security alerts from your hosting provider and software vendors. When major security issues on the scale of Heartbleed occur, hosting companies will engage with their customers and guide them through the patching process. Microsoft famously issues new patches every Tuesday (*patch Tuesday*) so make sure to sign up to its newsletter if you use Microsoft technology.

Software Tools

In addition to keeping your ear to the ground, automated tools can check your dependencies for known vulnerabilities. Node.js leads the way here, as the *Node Package Manager (NPM)* now incorporates the `npm audit` command that can be used to cross-check your dependency versions against an open source database of vulnerabilities. The equivalent tool for Ruby is the `bundler-audit` gem; for Java and .NET, the Open Web Application Security Project (OWASP) publishes a command line tool called `dependency-check`. Incorporating these tools into your build process will alert you of any potential vulnerabilities whenever your code is built and will allow you to assess the risks around each vulnerability.

Your source code repository can also help. GitHub automatically scans code hosted on their site, and will issue security alerts whenever vulnerable dependencies are found.

Know When to Upgrade

It's important to note that not all security issues merit equal priority! Constantly upgrading your dependencies can be time-consuming, especially since many of the security concerns in a particular advisory may be mitigated in your system by other factors. Large organizations have formal processes for reviewing security alerts, prioritizing them, and then choosing the appropriate action. It's perfectly acceptable to fold in minor security upgrades at the next scheduled release, as long as your team has assessed the risks involved.

Securing Configuration

Software is only as secure as it is configured to be. This is particularly true of third-party software: if you install a new database and start running with the default user account and password, you will quickly run into trouble. Hackers frequently scan the internet for software components running with their default settings, since they know that many site owners will neglect to customize their configurations when installing software.

If you are running software with an unsecured configuration, you are probably advertising this fact to the world. The information security consulting group Offensive Security hosts the Google Hacking Database, a listing of insecure software you can find via a simple Google search. The Google search spider does a thorough job of indexing pages on the web and offers a powerful set of tools for refining searches based on this information. For example, googling *index of /etc/certs* will list millions of web servers that expose their digital certificate directories to the world— a major security flaw!

Deploying your dependencies with a secure configuration is absolutely key to not getting hacked. A secure configuration requires setting up your services with strong credentials, storing your configuration information securely, and limiting the damage an attacker can do if they gain access to one part of your environment. Let's see how.

Disable Default Credentials

Many software packages come with default login credentials to make them easy for a first-time user to get up and running. Make sure you disable these credentials before deploying the software to test or production environments. If your database, web server, or content management system is deployed with, for example, an `admin` account, it will be quickly detected by bots scanning the internet for vulnerable software.

Disable Open Directory Listings

Web servers tend to overshare. Older versions of the Apache web server, for instance, map URL paths to files, and will helpfully list the files a directory contains if the filename was omitted in the URL. *Open directory listings* invite hackers to explore your filesystem, allowing them to search for sensitive data files and security keys. Make sure to disable directory listings in your web server configuration. Listing 14-4 shows how this is done in the Apache web server.

```
<Directory /var/www/>
   Options Indexes FollowSymLinks
   AllowOverride None
   Require all granted
</Directory>
```

Listing 14-4: Remove the keyword Indexes to prevent this Apache configuration file from generating open directory listings.

Protect Your Configuration Information

Your web server configuration will likely contain sensitive information, such as database credentials and API keys. Many development teams store configuration files in source control, to make deployment easier. However, consider what a hacker could do with access to your source control system: this type of sensitive information is the first thing hackers will search for. Database credentials, API keys, private encryption keys, certificates, and other sensitive configuration details need to be kept *externally* from source control.

One common approach is to record sensitive configuration in environmental variables at the operating system level, and have your configuration code initialize itself from these environmental variables when it starts up. These environmental variables can be initialized by configuration files stored locally on the server.

Another approach is to use a dedicated configuration store. Amazon Web Services (AWS) allows you to store configuration securely in its Systems Manager Parameter Store. Microsoft servers frequently store credentials in Active Directory, which allows for fine-grained permissions. Storing configuration in a database table is another option, though you should consider how an attacker may be able to escalate an attack if they gain access to your database. (Your web server will also have to access your database credentials before it can load the rest of the configuration!)

One surefire way to secure configuration information is to store it in encrypted form, encrypted with an algorithm such as AES-128. This approach means that a hacker will have to compromise your configuration data *and* your decryption key before they can steal your credentials. Just remember to store the decryption key in a different location from the configuration files, or the security benefit is neglible.

Harden Test Environments

Preproduction environments typically have the same software installed as their production counterparts but are frequently less secure. If your test environment contains sensitive data—for instance, if you ever copy data from the production environment to help with testing—you need to configure your test environments to be just as secure as your production environment. Crucially, production and nonproduction should not share credentials or API keys; it's important that you limit the damage a hacker can do if they manage to compromise your test server.

Secure Administrative Frontends

Some software components come with administrative tools that are available over the internet. Administrative interfaces are a favorite target for hackers. You will often encounter malicious bots probing for unsecured WordPress instances by testing for the presence of a */wp-login.php* page, for instance.

If you don't intend to use these administrative frontends, disable them in your configuration. If you do intend to use them, make sure to remove any default login credentials, and, if possible, restrict the IP range that can access them. Consult the documentation for your software stack or do a quick search on Stack Overflow (*https://stackoverflow.com/*) to find out how.

Now that you have learned how to secure third-party code running on your servers, let's look at how to securely integrate with code running on other people's servers.

Securing the Services That You Use

Third-party services are widely used in modern web development. You might be using Facebook Login for authentication, Google AdSense to place advertisements on your site, Akamai for hosting static content, SendGrid for sending transactional email, and Stripe for processing payments.

Integrating these kinds of services into your website generally means creating an account with the service provider, being supplied secret access credentials, and altering your website code to make use of the service. Two security considerations arise here. First, hackers will often attempt to steal your access credentials in order to access your account with these services. This will allow them to mine information about your users, for instance, or even to initiate financial transactions in the case of payment processors. Second, every third-party service is a potential attack vector to your site, because hackers try to compromise service providers in order to get access to a broad range of targets.

Let's start with the first consideration: learning how to safely store your access credentials.

Protect Your API Keys

Many third-party services issue you an application programming interface (API) key when you sign up, and your code must present the key as an access token when it interacts with the API. API keys need to be stored safely. Generally, this means storing the API key securely in the configuration on the server, as discussed in the previous section.

Some APIs issue *two* API keys: a *public key* that can be safely passed to the browser, used to make API calls from JavaScript; and a *private key* that must be kept securely on the server, used to make private API calls from the server side for more-sensitive actions. The public key has fewer privileges associated with it. Audit your code to make sure these keys don't get mixed up! You don't want to accidentally send the higher-privilege private key to the client. Even something as simple as naming your configuration variables SECRET_KEY will remind your development team of the risks.

Other services allow you to generate a temporary access token that can be passed to the client. Typically, these tokens can be used only once, or within a limited time window, to prevent abuse by a malicious user. These access tokens protect against *replay attacks*, whereby an attacker resends HTTP requests in an attempt to repeat an action (for instance, to duplicate a payment). Make sure your code generates access tokens only when a user has already authenticated themselves, or an attacker may be able generate new access tokens on demand.

Secure Your Webhooks

Most API integrations involve making HTTPS calls from your web server or the browser, to the service provider's API. When a service provider needs to make calls in the opposite direction (for instance, to send you notifications), it may ask you to implement a *webhook*. This is a simple "reverse API" on your website that the service provider will send HTTPS requests to when an event happens. You might, for instance, get webhook calls when a user opens an email you sent or when your payment processor initiates a payment.

Since they are public URLs, webhooks can be called by anyone on the internet, not just the service provider. If the service provider supports sending credentials with a webhook invocation, you should verify that these credentials are correct before processing the webhook call.

If a webhook invocation is purely informational and contains no sensitive data, it may be sent with no credentials attached whatsoever. In this scenario, an attacker can easily spoof such webhook calls. Be prepared to verify the notification with a further callback to the service provider's API before doing any further processing.

Secure Content Served by Third Parties

Finding a way to serve malicious content under someone else's domain is a favorite trick of hackers; victims can be lulled into a false sense of security by the sites they trust. Users have been conditioned to trust the padlock icon in the browser, so if a hacker can find a way to deploy malware under the security certificate of a large company, they will be able to trick more victims into downloading it.

Many websites use content delivery networks (CDNs) or cloud-based storage—such as Amazon S3—to serve frequently accessed content. When web developers integrate with this type of service, they often route traffic from their domain to the service by making DNS changes—for instance, by redirecting traffic on a subdomain such as *subdomain.example.com* to the service. This allows content served by the third party to be encrypted with the site's security certificate.

Hackers frequently attempt *subdomain takeovers* by scanning the internet for DNS entries describing subdomains that point to IP addresses for uninitialized or deactivated services. They will then register with the service provider and *squat* on one of the listed IP addresses. This will allow them to create links to their malicious content by using the domain of the victim.

If your website serves content hosted by a CDN or cloud-based storage, you need to be careful that your DNS entries point to only live IP addresses. Make DNS changes only after you have verified that the service is up and running under your control, and revoke DNS changes promptly if you change service providers.

Now that you know how to protect your integrations with service providers, let's look at threats in the other direction.

Services as an Attack Vector

Third-party services are potentially a vector for malicious attacks *against* your website. This is particularly true of services you integrate on the client side, because any JavaScript you import from a third-party domain comes with security risks.

Let's use Google Analytics as an example. When you add the Google Analytics tool to your site, you register for an account with Google to get a tracking ID and then import external JavaScript on pages where you wish to track user activity, as shown in Listing 14-5.

```
<script src="https://www.googletagmanager.com/gtag/js?id=GA_TRACKING_ID"></script>
```

Listing 14-5: The recipe for adding Google Analytics to your web pages

The imported code can read anything in the page's DOM, including sensitive data the user types in. It will also be able to make changes to the DOM in potentially misleading ways; for example, in order to trick the user into entering their credentials. It's important to consider these risks as you add client-side services. Malicious code can be served by the third-party service itself or by an attacker that has compromised the service. (In case you are wondering: Google Analytics has never been compromised by an attacker. I am simply using it as an example here!)

Unfortunately, the browser security model is not currently very sophisticated when considering how to run client-side code imported from third parties. JavaScript code *within* a browser runs in a *sandbox*, meaning it is isolated from the underlying operating system and can't access files on disk, but JavaScript files imported from *different* sources on a web page all play in the same sandbox.

The upcoming web components specification (*https://www.webcomponents .org/*), currently being developed by the HTML standards committee, defines more-granular permissions for code and page elements. While these details are being finalized and implemented, however, you should implement sensible security precautions on your site. Let's discuss how to secure your client-side integrations, by looking at what is (by far) the most common vector for attacks via a third-party channel: *malvertising*.

Be Wary of Malvertising

Advertising is a major part of the modern web: much of the content on the internet is funded by advertising revenue, and companies spend more than $100 billion annually on online advertisements. Advertisements are usually placed on websites by third-party ad platforms. A site owner (referred to as a *publisher* in the online advertising world) will subscribe to the ad platform and then demarcate various areas of their site as places advertisements should appear. The ad platform will populate these spaces as the site loads, using JavaScript imported directly on each page.

Major ad platforms such as Google AdSense use analytics to identify the type of content a publisher is hosting, and the type of people who visit the site, in order to determine the types of advertising to place. Publishers sometimes deal with advertisers directly, or have their ad spaces placed on an *exchange*, whereby ad buyers purchase *blocks* of ads. (An ad buyer might purchase 1,000 ad impressions for a particular demographic such as *men aged 18–25 who visit sneaker sites*.)

As a publisher, you have some control over the advertisements you carry, but generally do not get to approve each one beforehand. Google AdSense, for example, allows publishers to block categories of ads or specific web domains, or to reject specific ads after they have already begun to be shown to users.

This is a security risk because hackers frequently use ad platforms as an attack vector. Malicious ads—*malvertising*—allow an attacker to target many sites at once with malware. Malvertising is an increasingly common threat on the internet that can embarrass publishers and ad networks, and make victims out of their users.

Avoid Malware Delivery

Malware in advertising is typically delivered via *exploit kits*, which determine whether a particular browser and operating system is vulnerable before delivering the actual malicious code: the *payload*. Payloads can include scripts that redirect or lock the browser, viruses or ransomware delivered via vulnerabilities in plug-ins, or even JavaScript code that mines cryptocurrency in the user's browser.

Exploit kit authors are in an arms race with security researchers. To avoid detection, exploit kits are hosted at dynamically generated URLs and avoid automated scans by triggering only sporadically. Exploit kits have even been observed trying to prevent malware analysis by detecting when they are running in a virtual machine (malware researchers often use virtual machines to quarantine harmful code as they analyze it).

If your users are being hit by malware delivered through ads on your site, you are putting them in danger. You can protect them by making sure you partner with only trustworthy ad platforms, deploying ads in secure frames in your web pages, and continually being on the lookout for malicious ads.

Use a Reputable Ad Platform

For the most part, defending against malvertising is the responsibility of the ad platform. They are the ones who have the relationship with the ad buyers, and only they have enough visibility across those advertisers to spot malicious actors.

Google is (by far) the biggest player in the advertising space. Google permits smaller publishers to monetize their sites by using the self-service AdSense platform. Larger publishers are granted access to AdX, a platform that allows a publisher to specify their advertising partners and set their own prices. Both platforms take ads from third-party advertising networks.

Google is remarkably on the ball about defending against malicious ads, since so much of their revenue depends on their advertising platform. To take advantage of this, you should make AdSense or AdX your first choice when choosing an ad platform.

Google chooses not to work with some types of sites, however, for reputational reasons. You will have a hard time getting approved for AdSense if you host adult-themed or violent content, for instance. In this scenario, you may have to work with a smaller advertising platform that will likely have fewer resources and less inclination to secure you against malware. Do your research before picking a platform.

Use SafeFrame

The most effective way of isolating third-party content in a web page is to host that content inside an `<iframe>` tag. JavaScript code loaded inside an iframe (*inline frame*) cannot access the DOM of the containing page. HTML5 adds even more granular controls by adding the `sandbox` attribute to the `<iframe>` tag. This attribute allows the frame to specify whether the contained content can, for example, submit `POST` requests or open new windows.

The advertising industry has adopted a standard called *SafeFrame*, which allows publishers to specify that ads must be run in an iframe. The SafeFrame standard uses `<iframe>` tags, and adds a JavaScript API that allows the advertiser to overcome some of the native limitations of iframes. The

API permits advertising scripts to know when the frame is visible and to respond to size changes, for instance.

Your advertising platform will have an option to show *only* SafeFrame-compliant ads, and you should choose that option. This will stop any malicious ad scripts that attempt to interfere with the web page as it is rendered.

Tailor Your Ad Preferences

Most advertising platforms allow you to customize the type of ad content you show to users. If you use Google AdSense, make sure you show content from only Google certified ad networks. Hackers have been known to buy expired domains for smaller, defunct ad networks in order to deliver malware.

Take stock of what categories of ads you are showing too. You probably want to block advertisements for get-rich-quick schemes and multilevel marketing campaigns, as well as anything that describes itself as a downloadable utility.

Review and Report Suspicious Ads

Periodically review the ads being shown on your site from within your ad platform dashboard. (Remember: ads are tailored to the visitor, so simply visiting your site in a browser won't show you the full range of ads being shown.) Report and block anything that looks suspicious. It is also a good idea to log outgoing URLs as users leave your site, so you can track whether any ads you are hosting are taking users to suspicious sites.

Summary

Vulnerabilities in third-party code are a threat to your website. Use a dependency manager to keep track of what third-party dependencies you use, keep your dependency inventory under source control, and name explicit dependency versions. Make sure your build and deployment processes are scripted, so it is easy to upgrade your dependencies when security advisories are issued. (This should include operating system patches.) Stay engaged with social media and news sites so you know when security advisories are issued. Use auditing tools to detect vulnerable software components in your dependency tree. Use the `integrity` attribute when importing JavaScript on your web pages so these files can be validated by the browser.

Make sure you are not running with an insecure configuration; hackers will discover insecure software components by using simple Google searches. Disable any default credentials for your system, and disable open directory listings in your web server configuration. Keep sensitive configuration details (for example, database access credentials or API keys) out of source control; instead, keep them in a dedicated configuration store and load them at startup. Take care to secure configuration for test environments and administrative frontends, since they are common targets for hackers.

Be careful not to pass sensitive API keys or access tokens to the client. Secure any webhooks against spoofing attacks. If you serve content hosted from other locations under your domain—say, by hosting it on a content delivery network or in cloud storage—make sure an attacker is not able to put malware on those systems and serve it under your security certificate.

Know the risks around malware delivered by any ads you host on your site. Use a reputable ad network and take advantage of all the SafeFrame-based security settings it permits. Periodically review the ads being placed on your site. Report any ads you find suspicious and blacklist them.

In the next chapter, you will look at vulnerabilities related to XML parsing. XML is a ubiquitous part of the modern internet and a common target for hackers looking to compromise your system.

15

XML ATTACKS

With the explosive growth of the internet in the '90s, organizations began sharing data with each other over the web. Sharing data between computers meant agreeing on a shared data format. Human-readable documents on the web were being marked up with HyperText Markup Language (HTML). Machine-readable files were often stored in an analogous data format called *Extensible Markup Language (XML)*.

XML can be thought of as a more general implementation of HTML: in this form of markup, the tag and attribute names can be chosen by the document author rather than being fixed, as they are in the HTML specification. In Listing 15-1, you can see an XML file describing a catalog of books, using tags like <catalog>, <book>, and <author>.

```
<?xml version="1.0"?>
<catalog>
    <book id="7991728882998">
        <author>Sponden, Phillis</author>
        <title>The Evil Horse That Knew Karate</title>
        <genre>Young Adult Fiction</genre>
        <description>Three teenagers with very different personalities
team up to defeat a surprising villain.</description>
    </book>
    <book id="28299171927772">
        <author>Chenoworth, Dr. Sebastian</author>
        <title>Medical Encyclopedia of Elbows, 12th Edition</title>
        <genre>Medical</genre>
        <description>The world's foremost forearm expert gives detailed diagnostic
and clinical advice on maintaining everyone's favorite joint.</description>
    </book>
</catalog>
```

Listing 15-1: An XML document describing a catalog of books

The popularity of this data format, especially in the early days of the web, means that XML *parsing*—the process of turning an XML file into in-memory code objects—has been implemented in every browser and web server of the past few decades. Unfortunately, XML parsers are a common target for hackers. Even if your site doesn't handle XML by design, your web server may parse the data format by default. This chapter shows how XML parsers can be attacked and how to defuse these attacks.

The Uses of XML

Much like HTML, XML encloses data items between tags and allows tags to be embedded within one another. The author of an XML document can choose semantically meaningful tag names so that the XML document is self-describing. Because XML is very readable, the data format was widely adopted to encode data for consumption by other applications.

The uses of XML are many. Application programming interfaces (APIs) that allow client software to call functions over the internet frequently accept and respond using XML. JavaScript code in web pages that communicates asynchronously back to the server often uses XML. Many types of applications—web servers included—use XML-based configuration files.

In the past decade, some of these applications have started using better-suited, less verbose data formats than XML. For example, JSON is a more natural method of encoding data in JavaScript and other scripting languages. The YAML language uses meaningful indentation, making it a simpler format for configuration files. Nevertheless, every web server implements XML parsing in some fashion and needs to be secured against XML attacks.

XML vulnerabilities generally occur during the validation process. Let's take a minute to discuss what validation means in the context of parsing an XML document.

Validating XML

Since the author of an XML file is able to choose which tag names are used in the document, any application reading the data needs to know which tags to expect and in what order they will appear. The expected structure of an XML document is often described by a formal grammar against which the document can be *validated*.

A *grammar* file dictates to a parser which sequences of characters are valid expressions within the language. A programming language grammar might specify, for instance, that variable names can contain only alphanumeric characters, and that certain operators like + require two inputs.

XML has two major ways of describing the expected structure of an XML document. A *document type definition (DTD)* file resembles the *Bachus–Naur Form (BNF)* notation often used to describe programming language grammars. An *XML Schema Definition (XSD)* file is a more modern, more expressive alternative, capable of describing a wider set of XML documents; in this case, the grammar itself is described in an XML file. Both methods of XML validation are widely supported by XML parsers. However, DTDs contain a couple of features that can expose the parser to attack, so that's what we'll focus on.

Document Type Definitions

A DTD file describes the structure of an XML file by specifying the tags, subtags, and types of data expected in a document. Listing 15-2 shows a DTD file describing the expected structure of the <catalog> and <book> tags in Listing 15-1.

```
<!DOCTYPE catalog [
  <!ELEMENT catalog      (book+)>
  <!ELEMENT book         (author,title,genre,description)>
  <!ENTITY  author       (#PCDATA)>
  <!ENTITY  title        (#PCDATA)>
  <!ENTITY  genre        (#PCDATA)>
  <!ENTITY  description  (#PCDATA)>
  <!ATTLIST book id CDATA>
]>
```

Listing 15-2: A DTD file describing the format of the XML in Listing 15-1

This DTD describes that the top-level <catalog> tag is expected to contain zero or more <book> tags (the quantity is denoted by the + sign), and that each <book> tag is expected to contain tags describing the author, title, genre, and description, plus an id attribute. The tags and attribute are expected to contain parsed character data (#PCDATA) or character data (CDATA)—that is, text rather than tags.

DTDs can be included within an XML document to make the document self-validating. However, a parser that supports such *inline* DTDs is vulnerable to attack—because a malicious user uploading such an XML document has control over the contents of the DTD, rather than it being supplied by the parser itself. Hackers have used inline DTDs to exponentially increase the amount of server memory a document consumes during parsing (an XML bomb), and access to other files on the server (an XML external entity attack). Let's see how these attacks work.

XML Bombs

An *XML bomb* uses an inline DTD to explode the memory usage of an XML parser. This will take a web server offline by exhausting all the memory available to the server and causing it to crash.

XML bombs take advantage of the fact that DTDs can specify simple string substitution macros that are expanded at parse time, called *internal entity declarations*. If a snippet of text is frequently used in an XML file, you can declare it in the DTD as an internal entity. That way, you don't have to type it out every time you need it in the document—you just type the entity name as a shorthand. In Listing 15-3, an XML file containing employee records specifies the company name in the DTD by using an internal entity declaration.

```
<?xml version="1.0"?>
<!DOCTYPE employees [
  <!ELEMENT employees (employee)*>
  <!ELEMENT employee (#PCDATA)>
  <!ENTITY company "Rock and Gravel Company"❶>
]>
<employees>
  <employee>
    Fred Flintstone, &company;❷
  </employee>
  <employee>
    Barney Rubble, &company;❸
  </employee>
</employees>
```

Listing 15-3: An internal entity declaration

The string &company; ❷❸ acts as a placeholder for the value Rock and Gravel Company ❶. When the document is parsed, the parser replaces all instances of &company; with Rock and Gravel Company and produces the final document shown in Listing 15-4.

```
<?xml version="1.0"?>
<employees>
  <employee>
    Fred Flintstone, Rock and Gravel Company
  </employee>
  <employee>
    Barney Rubble, Rock and Gravel Company
  </employee>
</employees>
```

Listing 15-4: The XML document after the parser processes the DTD

Internal entity declarations are useful, if seldom used. Problems occur when internal entity declarations refer to other internal entity declarations. Listing 15-5 shows a nested series of entity declarations that constitute an XML bomb.

```
<?xml version="1.0"?>
<!DOCTYPE lolz [
  <!ENTITY lol "lol">
  <!ENTITY lol2 "&lol;&lol;&lol;&lol;&lol;&lol;&lol;&lol;&lol;&lol;">
  <!ENTITY lol3 "&lol2;&lol2;&lol2;&lol2;&lol2;&lol2;&lol2;&lol2;&lol2;&lol2;">
  <!ENTITY lol4 "&lol3;&lol3;&lol3;&lol3;&lol3;&lol3;&lol3;&lol3;&lol3;&lol3;">
  <!ENTITY lol5 "&lol4;&lol4;&lol4;&lol4;&lol4;&lol4;&lol4;&lol4;&lol4;&lol4;">
  <!ENTITY lol6 "&lol5;&lol5;&lol5;&lol5;&lol5;&lol5;&lol5;&lol5;&lol5;&lol5;">
  <!ENTITY lol7 "&lol6;&lol6;&lol6;&lol6;&lol6;&lol6;&lol6;&lol6;&lol6;&lol6;">
  <!ENTITY lol8 "&lol7;&lol7;&lol7;&lol7;&lol7;&lol7;&lol7;&lol7;&lol7;&lol7;">
  <!ENTITY lol9 "&lol8;&lol8;&lol8;&lol8;&lol8;&lol8;&lol8;&lol8;&lol8;&lol8;">
]>
<lolz>&lol9;</lolz>
```

Listing 15-5: A type of XML bomb known as the billion laughs attack

When this XML file is parsed, the &lol9; string is replaced with 10 occurrences of the string &lol8;. Then *each* occurrence of &lol8; is replaced with 10 occurrences of the string &lol7;. The final form of the XML file consists of a `<lolz>` tag containing over a *billion* occurrences of the string lol. This simple XML file will take up over 3GB of memory when the DTD is fully expanded, enough to crash the XML parser!

Exhausting the memory available to the XML parser will take your web server offline, which makes XML bombs an effective way for a hacker to launch a denial-of-service attack. All an attacker needs to do is to find a URL on your site that accepts XML uploads, and they can take you offline with a click of a button.

XML parsers that accept inline DTDs are also vulnerable to a sneakier type of attack that takes advantage of entity definitions in a different manner.

XML External Entity Attacks

DTDs can include content from external files. If an XML parser is configured to process inline DTDs, an attacker can use these *external entity declarations* to explore the local filesystem or to trigger network requests from the web server itself.

A typical external entity looks like Listing 15-6.

```
<?xml version="1.0" standalone="no"?>
<!DOCTYPE copyright [
  <!ELEMENT copyright (#PCDATA)>
  <!ENTITY copy PUBLIC "http://www.w3.org/xmlspec/copyright.xml"❶>
]>
<copyright>&copy;❷ </copyright>
```

Listing 15-6: Using an external entity to include boilerplate copyright text in an XML file

According to the XML 1.0 specification, a parser is expected to read the contents of the file specified in the external entity and insert that data into the XML document wherever the entity is referenced. In this example, the data hosted at *http://www.w3.org/xmlspec/copyright.xml* ❶ would be inserted into the XML document wherever the text © ❷ appears.

The URL referenced by the external entity declaration can use various network protocols, depending on the prefix. Our example DTD uses the *http://* prefix, which will cause the parser to make an HTTP request. The XML specification also supports reading local files on disk, using the *file://* prefix. For this reason, external entity definitions are a security *disaster*.

How Hackers Exploit External Entities

When an XML parser throws an error, the error message will often include the contents of the XML document being parsed. Knowing this, hackers use external entity declarations to read files on a server. A maliciously crafted XML file might include a reference to a file such as *file://etc/passwd* on a Linux system, for instance. When this external file is inserted into the XML document by the parser, the XML becomes malformed—so parsing fails. The parser then dutifully includes the contents of the file in the error response, allowing the hacker to view the sensitive data within the referenced file. Using this technique, hackers can read sensitive files on a vulnerable web server that contain passwords and other confidential information.

External entities can also be used to commit *server-side request forgery (SSRF)* attacks, whereby an attacker triggers malicious HTTP requests from your server. A naïvely configured XML parser will make a network request whenever it encounters an external entity URL with a network protocol prefix. Being able to trick your web server into making a network request on a URL of their choosing is a boon for an attacker! Hackers have used this feature to probe internal networks, to launch denial-of-service attacks on third parties, and to disguise malicious URL calls. You will learn more about the risks around SSRF attacks in the next chapter.

Securing Your XML Parser

This is a simple fix to protect your parser from XML attacks: disable the processing of inline DTDs in your configuration. DTDs are a legacy technology, and inline DTDs are a bad idea, period. In fact, many modern XML parsers are hardened by default, meaning out of the box they disable features that allow the parser to be attacked, so you might be protected already. If you are unsure, you should check what (if any) XML parsing technology you are using.

The following sections describe how to secure your XML parser in some of the major web programming languages. Even if you think your code doesn't parse XML, the third-party dependencies you use likely use XML in some form. Make sure you analyze your entire dependency tree to see what libraries are loaded into memory when your web server starts up.

Python

The `defusedxml` library explicitly rejects inline DTDs and is a drop-in replacement for Python's standard XML parsing library. Use this module in place of Python's standard library.

Ruby

The de facto standard for parsing XML in Ruby is the `Nokogiri` library. This library has been hardened to XML attacks since version 1.5.4, so make sure your code uses that version or higher for parsing.

Node.js

Node.js has a variety of modules for parsing XML, including `xml2js`, `parse-xml`, and `node-xml`. Most of them omit processing of DTDs by design, so make sure to consult the documentation for the parser you use.

Java

Java has a variety of methods of parsing XML. Parsers that adhere to Java specifications typically initiate parsing via the class `javax.xml.parsers.Document BuilderFactory`. Listing 15-7 illustrates how to configure secure XML parsing in this class wherever it is instantiated, using the `XMLConstants.FEATURE_SECURE _PROCESSING` feature.

```
DocumentBuilderFactory factory = DocumentBuilderFactory.newInstance();
factory.setFeature(XMLConstants.FEATURE_SECURE_PROCESSING, true);
```

Listing 15-7: Securing a Java XML parsing library

.NET

.NET has a variety of methods of parsing XML, all contained in the `System .Xml` namespace. `XmlDictionaryReader`, `XmlNodeReader`, and `XmlReader` are safe by default, as are `System.Xml.Linq.XElement` and `System.Xml.Linq.XDocument`. `System .Xml.XmlDocument`, `System.Xml.XmlTextReader`, and `System.Xml.XPath.XPathNavigator` have been secured since .NET version 4.5.2. If you are using an earlier version of .NET, you should switch to a secure parser, or disable the processing of inline DTDs. Listing 15-8 shows how to do this by setting the `ProhibitDtd` attribute flag.

```
XmlTextReader reader = new XmlTextReader(stream);
reader.ProhibitDtd = true;
```

Listing 15-8: Disabling processing of inline DTDs in .NET

Other Considerations

The threat of external entity attacks illustrates the importance of following the *principle of least privilege*, which states that software components and processes should be granted the minimal set of permissions required to perform their tasks. There is rarely a good reason for an XML parser to make outbound network requests: consider locking down outbound network requests for your web server as a whole. If you do need outbound network access—for example, if your server code calls third-party APIs—you should whitelist the domains of those APIs in your firewall rules.

Similarly, it's important to restrict the directories on disk that your web server can access. On the Linux operating system, this can be achieved by running your web server process in a chroot jail that ignores any attempts by the running process to change its root directory. On the Windows operating system, you should manually whitelist the directories that the web server can access.

Summary

Extensible Markup Language (XML) is a flexible data format widely used to exchange machine-readable data on the internet. Your XML parser may be vulnerable to attack if it is configured to accept and process inline document type definitions (DTDs). XML bombs use inline DTDs to explode the parser's memory use, potentially crashing your web server. XML external entity attacks reference local files or network addresses, and can be used to trick the parser into revealing sensitive information or make malicious network requests. Make sure you use a hardened XML parser that disables inline DTD parsing.

The next chapter expands on a concept touched on in this chapter: how security flaws in your web server can be leveraged by hackers to launch attacks on third parties. Even when you aren't the victim directly, it's important to be a good internet citizen and stop attacks that use your system.

16

DON'T BE AN ACCESSORY

Malicious actors have a lot of places to hide on the internet. Hackers routinely impersonate other people and use compromised servers to evade detection. This chapter explores various ways that your web presence may be helping attackers get away with malicious acts, even when you aren't the target of their attacks.

Making sure you aren't being an accessory will win you good internet citizen points. More practically, if hackers are using your system as a jumping-off point for attacking others, you will quickly find your domain and IP addresses getting blacklisted from key services, and you may even end up being cut off by your hosting provider.

This chapter covers several vulnerabilities that can make you an accessory to malicious acts on the internet. The first couple of vulnerabilities are used by hackers to send harmful emails: scammers frequently use *email address spoofing* to disguise who is sending an email, and use *open redirects* on websites to disguise malicious links in email.

Next, you'll see how your site can be hosted within a frame on someone else's page and be used as part of a *clickjacking* attack. In this type of attack, your site is used in a bait-and-switch scheme to trick users into clicking something harmful.

You saw in the preceding chapter how hackers can use vulnerabilities in XML parsers in order to trigger network requests. If an attacker can craft malicious HTTP requests that trigger outbound network access from your server, you are enabling *server-side request forgery* attacks. You will learn common ways this type of attack can be launched and how to protect against it.

Finally, you will look at the risk of malware being installed on your servers for use in a *botnet*. You may unknowingly be hosting zombie code that can be controlled remotely by an attacker!

Email Fraud

Email is sent using the *Simple Mail Transfer Protocol (SMTP)*. One major oversight in the original design of SMTP is that it does not have a mechanism for authentication: the sender of an email is able to attach *any* email address they want in the From header, and until relatively recently, there was no way for the receiving agent to verify that the sender is who they claim to be.

As a result, of course, we all receive massive amounts of spam email. Experts estimate that around *half* of all email sent is spam—nearly 15 billion spam emails are sent every day. Spam email generally contains unwanted (and often misleading) marketing material that is a nuisance to the recipient.

Related to spam email is *phishing* email: the sender attempts to trick the recipient into revealing sensitive personal information such as passwords or credit card details. A common trick is to email a victim with what looks like a password reset email for a website they use, but have the reset link to a *doppelganger domain*—a domain whose name looks superficially similar to the real domain name that hosts a fake version of the site. The fake site will harvest the user's credentials on behalf of the attacker, and then redirect the user to the real site so the victim is none the wiser.

An even more vicious form of this type of attack is *spearphishing*, whereby the content of a malicious email is tailored to a small audience. Fraudsters sending this type of email often conduct detailed research on their victims in order to be able to name-drop or impersonate colleagues. *CEO fraud*—through which a scammer pretends to be a C-level officer and emails another employee to request a wire transfer—netted hackers over $26 billion between 2016 and 2019 according to the FBI. And that's just counting the victims who reported the loss to law enforcement.

Thankfully, mail service providers have developed sophisticated algorithms for detecting spam and phishing email. Gmail, for instance, will scan each incoming email and quickly decide whenever it is legitimate, sending anything that looks suspicious to the junk folder. Spam filters use many inputs when classifying email: keywords in the email and the subject line, the email domain, and the presence of any suspicious outgoing links in the body of the mail.

Your website and organization likely send email from a custom domain, so the onus is on *you* to prevent your email from being marked as spam and to protect your users from malicious email that pretends to be from your domain. You have a couple of ways to do this: by implementing a Sender Policy Framework and by using DomainKeys Identified Mail when you generate email.

Implement a Sender Policy Framework

Implementing a *Sender Policy Framework (SPF)* entails whitelisting the IP addresses that are authorized to send email from your web domain in the DNS. Because SMTP sits on top of the TCP, the IP address that an email is sent from cannot be spoofed in the same way as the From header. By explicitly whitelisting IP addresses in your domain name records, mail receiving agents will be able to verify that incoming mail originated from a permitted source.

Listing 16-1 shows how to specify a Sender Policy Framework in your DNS records.

```
v=spf1❶ ip4:192.0.2.0/24 ip4:198.51.100.123❷ a❸ -all❹
```

Listing 16-1: A DNS record to whitelist a range of IP addresses authorized to send email from a given domain as part of your SPF

This record would be added as a *.txt* record in your domain name records. In this syntax, the v= argument ❶ defines the version of SPF used. The ip4 ❷ and a ❸ flags specify the systems permitted to send messages for the given domain: in this case, a range of IP addresses, and the IP address corresponding to the domain (indicated by the a flag) itself. The -all flag ❹ at the end of the record tells mail providers that if the preceding mechanisms did not match, the message should be rejected.

Implement DomainKeys Identified Mail

DomainKeys can be used to generate a digital signature for outgoing mail, to prove an email was legitimately sent from your domain and that it wasn't modified in transit. *DomainKeys Identified Mail (DKIM)* uses public-key cryptography, signing outgoing messages from a domain with a private key and allowing recipients to validate the signature by using a public key hosted in DNS. Only the sender knows the private signing key, so only they can generate legitimate signatures. A mail receiving agent will recalculate the signature by combining the email's content and the public signing key hosted on your domain. If the recalculated signature does not match the signature attached to the mail, the email will be rejected.

To implement DKIM, you need to add a DomainKey in a *.txt* record to your domain. Listing 16-2 shows an example.

```
k=rsa; ❶ p=MIGfMA0GCSqGSIb3DQEBAQUAA4GNADCBiQKBgQDDmzRmJRQxLEuyYiyMg4suA ❷
```

Listing 16-2: A (public) domain key is hosted in the DNS system, and the corresponding private key needs to be shared with the application generating email for the domain.

In this example, k indicates the key type ❶, and p is the public key used to recalculate the signature ❷.

Securing Your Email: Practical Steps

Your organization likely generates email from multiple locations. Email sent to a user in response to their actions on your website—called transactional email—will be triggered by your web server software, and often is generated via email services such as SendGrid or Mailgun. Email written by hand will be sent either by a webmail service (for example, Gmail) or from email server software hosted on your network (for example, Microsoft Exchange or Postfix). Your team may also be using email marketing or newsletter services such as Mailchimp or TinyLetter to send email.

Consult the documentation of your service providers or email server to see how to generate and add the DNS entries needed to implement SPF and DKIM. In fact, you may *already* be using DKIM, because many transactional email and marketing services require you to add the relevant DNS entries when you sign up to the service. As you lock down IP ranges and domains as part of your SPF implementation, remember to consider *all* the software that is sending email from your domain!

Disguising Malicious Links in Email

Spam algorithms look for malicious links in email, and to support this, webmail providers keep up-to-date blacklists of domains that are known to be harmful. Scanning for links to such domains is a common and effective way to block dangerous email.

As such, scammers have had to come up with new tricks to disguise harmful links, to prevent their email from being flagged and sent directly to the junk folder. One way to do this is to use a URL-shortening service like Bitly, which will encode a URL in a shorter form and redirect the user when they visit the link. However, in the ever-escalating spam wars, email scanning algorithms now *unroll* links to known URL-shortening services and check whether the final destination is harmful.

Hackers have found a subtler way to disguise malicious links in email. If your website can be used to disguise a link to an arbitrary URL on the internet—if you implement an *open redirect* anywhere on your site—you may be helping hackers disguise malicious links in the same way as a URL-shortening service. Not only are you making your users vulnerable to phishing scams, but the *genuine* email you send is liable to be blacklisted by spam-detection algorithms.

Open Redirects

In HTTP, a *redirect* occurs when a web server responds with a 301 (temporary redirect) or 302 (permanent redirect) response code, and supplies a URL that the browser should navigate to instead. One of the most common uses of redirects is to send an unauthenticated user to the login page if they attempt to visit a site. In this scenario, the site typically issues a second redirect *back* to the original URL after the user has authenticated themselves.

To enable this second redirect, the web server has to remember the original destination as the user logs in. Frequently, this is done by encoding the final destination URL within a query parameter in the login URL. If a hacker can encode an arbitrary URL in this query parameter—in other words, if the second redirect can send the user to a whole different website on the internet—you have what is known as an *open redirect*.

Preventing Open Redirects

Most sites won't ever need to redirect to an external URL. If any part of your website encodes a URL within another URL for the purpose of redirecting the user to that destination, you should make sure that these encoded URLs are *relative* URLs rather than *absolute* URLs: encoded links should point within your site, rather than externally.

Relative URLs begin with a forward slash (/), which is easy to check for. Hackers have found a few ways to disguise absolute URLs to look like relative URLs, so your code needs to account for that. Listing 16-3 shows how to check that a URL is a relative URL via simple pattern-matching logic.

```
import re
def is_relative(url):
  return re.match(r"^\/[^\/\\]"❶, url)
```

Listing 16-3: A function to check that a link is relative (internal to a website), using a regular expression in Python

This pattern ❶ states that the URL must begin with a forward slash, and the following character must not be another forward slash or a backslash (\). The second character is checked to protect against URLs such as *//:www.google.com*, which are interpreted by browsers as absolute URLs; they will be automatically prefixed by *http* or *https* depending on what protocol the page is currently using.

Another approach to preventing open redirects is to avoid encoding URLs within query parameters *altogether*. If you are encoding a URL for an eventual redirect following login, consider dropping the URL in a temporary cookie instead of a query parameter. An attacker is unable to forge a cookie in a victim's browser quite as easily, so you will close the door to abusive linking.

Other Considerations

Some types of websites do require external links to be posted by users. For instance, if you run a social news site, your users will often post links to external URLs. If this applies to your site, use the *Google Safe Browsing* API to check each URL against a blacklist of harmful sites.

After you have secured your email and redirect code, it's important to make sure your web pages can't be wrapped in other people's malicious websites. Let's look at how to protect your users against clickjacking attacks.

Clickjacking

HTML permits a web page to contain another web page, by using an <iframe> tag. This allows content from different web domains to be mixed in a controlled fashion, because JavaScript running on the page within the frame cannot access the containing page. The <iframe> tags are commonly used to embed third-party content in a web page—OAuth and CAPTCHA widgets often use them to secure cookies.

As with anything useful on the internet, hackers have found ways to abuse <iframe> tags. Modern CSS allows page elements to be layered on top of each other using the z-index attribute; elements with a higher z-index will hide elements with a lower z-index and receive click events first. Page elements can also be made transparent using the opacity attribute. By combining these techniques, a hacker can position a transparent <div> over an <iframe> element, and then trick a victim into clicking whatever content is stored in the <div> rather than the underlying content they believe they are clicking.

This click-hijacking—*clickjacking*—has been used in a variety of ways. In some cases, victims have been tricked into switching on their webcam so the attacker can watch them remotely. Another variation of this technique is *likejacking*, whereby a victim is tricked into liking something on Facebook without their knowledge. Selling likes on the dark web for promotional purposes is a big money-spinner for a hacker.

Preventing Clickjacking

If you run a website, you should make sure your site isn't used as bait in a clickjacking attack. Most sites never need to be hosted in <iframe> tags, so you should tell the browser that directly. Modern browsers support the Content -Security-Policy header that allows the response from the server to specify that the page should have no frame-ancestors, as shown in Listing 16-4.

```
Content-Security-Policy: frame-ancestors 'none'
```

Listing 16-4: A header that tells the browser never to host your website in a frame

Implementing this policy tells the browser to never put your website in a frame.

If for some reason your site does need to be contained within an <iframe>, you should tell the browsers *which* sites are permitted to host such a frame. You can do this by using the same Content-Security-Policy header to specify that the website can be its own frame ancestor. Listing 16-5 shows how to use the keyword self to permit your site to host iframes pointing to other parts of the same site.

```
Content-Security-Policy: frame-ancestors 'self'
```

Listing 16-5: A header that permits a site to host iframes of itself

Finally, if you need third-party websites to be able to host your site in a frame, you can whitelist individual web domains, as shown in Listing 16-6.

```
Content-Security-Policy: frame-ancestors example.com google.com
```

Listing 16-6: A header that permits a site to be hosted in an iframe by example.com and google.com

Now that you've looked at how to protect against clickjacking, let's see how attackers will try to launch malicious network requests from your server.

Server-Side Request Forgery

Hackers making malicious HTTP requests often seek to disguise where those requests are launched from. For instance, denial-of-service attacks—covered in the next chapter—are more effective when coming from many different IP addresses. If your web server makes outgoing HTTP requests, and a hacker can control which URLs those requests are sent to, you are vulnerable to a server-side request forgery (SSRF) attack, and a hacker can use your server to send malicious requests.

There are some legitimate reasons to make outbound network requests from your server. If you use any kind of third-party API, these are typically made available as web services over HTTPS. You might, for example, use server-side APIs to send transactional email, index content for searching, record unexpected errors in an error-reporting system, or process payments. Problems occur, however, when an attacker is able to manipulate the server into calling a URL of their choosing.

Typically, SSRF vulnerabilities occur when the outbound URL of an HTTP request sent *from* the web server is insecurely constructed from a part of an HTTP request sent *to* the server. A hacker will check a site for SSRF vulnerabilities by *spidering* through it, navigating to every page, and using hacking tools to replace every HTTP parameter they encounter with a URL under their control. If they detect any HTTP requests to their trap URL, they know the requests must have been triggered from your server, and that you are vulnerable to SSRF.

Hackers will also check to see if any part of your site accepts XML content, and use XML external entity attacks in an attempt to commit SSRF. Chapter 15 discussed this attack vector.

Protecting Against Server-Side Forgery

You can protect yourself against server-side forgery at several levels. The first, and most important step, is to audit any parts of your code that make outbound HTTP requests. You will almost always know ahead of time which domains need to be invoked as part of API calls, so the construction of URLs for API calls should use web domains recorded in your configuration or code rather than coming from the client. One way of ensuring this is to use the *software development kit (SDK)* that is usually made freely available with most APIs.

Because you should be following the practice of defense in depth—protecting yourself from vulnerabilities in multiple, overlapping ways—it makes sense to install safeguards against SSRF at the network level too. Whitelisting the individual domains that you need access to in your firewall, and banning all others, is a good way to catch any security issues you may have overlooked during code review.

Finally, consider employing penetration testing to detect SSRF vulnerabilities in your code. This can be done by employing an external team to find vulnerabilities in your website or by using an automated online tool to do the same. Effectively, you will be using the same tools that hackers use to detect vulnerabilities, before they get the chance to do so themselves.

Botnets

Hackers are always looking for spare computing power to power their attacks. If a hacker manages to compromise your server, they will frequently install a *bot*—a piece of malware that they can control using remote commands. Most bots operate as part of a peer-to-peer network of individual bots—a *botnet*—that communicate with each other by using an encrypted protocol.

Bots are often used to infect regular consumer devices like laptops. Managing to install a bot on a server is big prize, however, because significantly more computing power will be available to the bot. Scammers will pay a good price on the dark web for access keys that allow them to control botnets. They commonly use this spare computing power to mine bitcoin or commit *click fraud*—that is, artificially inflate page-view numbers of websites. Botnets are also used to generate spam email or to commit denial-of-service attacks (covered in the next chapter).

Protecting Against Malware Infection

Clearly, you want to avoid having any bot malware installed on the server. Chapter 6 discussed command injection and file upload vulnerabilities that could allow a hacker to install a bot on your server. Make sure you follow that chapter's advice to secure such vulnerabilities.

Additionally, you should also proactively protect your servers from infections. Running up-to-date antivirus software will help you quickly spot any kind of malware. Monitoring your outgoing network access will highlight suspicious activity: installed bots will periodically poll other IPs looking for other bots. You should also consider running an *integrity checker* on your web servers—a piece of software that checks for unexpected file changes on sensitive directories.

If you are using virtualized services or containers, you have an advantage here: any rebuild of the system will typically wipe away malicious software that was installed. Rebuilding from an image periodically will do a lot to keep your system safe from bot infestations.

Summary

Avoid being an accessory to attacks on others on the internet by doing the following:

- Protect the email you send by implementing SPF and DKIM headers in your domain name records.
- Make sure you have no open redirects on your site.
- Prevent your site from being hosted in an `<iframe>` tag by setting a content security policy.
- Audit your code to ensure that the server cannot be tricked into sending HTTP requests to an external URL of an attacker's choosing, and whitelist outbound network access to avoid being used in server-side request forgery attacks.
- Use virtualized servers, virus scanners, or vulnerability scanning tools to check for and remove bots.

In the next chapter, you will look at a brute-force technique that hackers can use to take your web server offline: the denial-of-service attack.

17

DENIAL-OF-SERVICE ATTACKS

 On October 21, 2016, internet users woke up and found that many of their favorite websites were inaccessible: Twitter, Spotify, Netflix, GitHub, Amazon, and many others all appeared to be offline. The root cause was an attack against a DNS provider. A massive wave of DNS lookup requests had brought the popular DNS provider Dyn to its knees. It took most of the day—during which two more huge waves of DNS lookups occurred—before services were fully restored.

The scale and impact of the outage were unprecedented. (The only incident of comparable impact occurred when a shark chomped through an undersea internet cable and the whole of Vietnam went offline for a while.) It was, however, just the latest incarnation of the common and increasingly dangerous *denial-of-service (DoS)* attack.

A denial-of-service attack is different from most types of vulnerabilities discussed in this book, as the intent of the attack isn't to compromise a system or website: the intent is to simply make it unavailable to other users. Generally, this is achieved by flooding the site with inbound traffic, so all server resources are exhausted. This chapter breaks down some of the more common techniques used in denial-of-service attacks and presents various ways to defend against them.

Denial-of-Service Attack Types

Responding to a network request generally requires more processing power than sending one. When a web server handles an HTTP request, for example, it has to parse the request, run database queries, write data to the logs, and construct the HTML to be returned. The user agent simply has to generate the request containing three pieces of information: the HTTP verb, the IP address it is being sent to, and the URL. Hackers use this asymmetry to overwhelm servers with network requests so they are unable to respond to legitimate users.

Hackers have discovered ways to launch denial-of-service attacks at every level of the network stack, not just over HTTP. Given how successful they have been in the past, many more methods will likely be discovered in the future. Let's look at some of the tools in an attacker's toolkit.

Internet Control Message Protocol Attacks

The *Internet Control Message Protocol (ICMP)* is used by servers, routers, and command line tools to check whether a network address is online. The protocol is simple: a request is transmitted to an IP address, and if the responding server is online, it will send back a confirmation that it is online. If you have ever used the ping utility to check whether a server is accessible, you have used ICMP under the hood.

ICMP is the simplest of the internet protocols, so inevitably, it was the first to be used in malicious ways. A *ping flood* attempts to overwhelm a server by sending an endless stream of ICMP requests, and can be initiated simply by a few lines of code. A slightly more sophisticated attack is the *ping of death* attack, which sends corrupt ICMP packets in an attempt to crash a server. This type of attack takes advantage of older software that does not correctly do bounds checking in incoming ICMP packets.

Transmission Control Protocol Attacks

Most ICMP-based attacks can be defused by modern network interfaces, so attackers have moved higher up the network stack to the TCP, which underpins most internet communication.

A TCP conversation begins with the TCP client sending a SYN (synchronize) message to the server, which is then expected to reply with a SYN-ACK (synchronize acknowledgement) response. The client should then complete the handshake by sending a final ACK message to the server. By flooding a server with SYN messages—a *SYN flood*—without completing the TCP handshake, hacking tools leave a server with a large number of "half-open" connections, exhausting the connection pool for legitimate clients. Then, when a legitimate client attempts to connect, the server rejects the connection.

Application Layer Attacks

Application layer attacks against a web server abuse the HTTP protocol. The *Slowloris* attack opens many HTTP connections to a server, and keeps those connections open by periodically sending partial HTTP requests, thus exhausting the server's connection pool. The *R-U-Dead-Yet? (RUDY)* attack sends never-ending POST requests to a server, with arbitrarily long Content-Length header values, to keep the server busy reading meaningless data.

Hackers have also found ways to take web servers offline by exploiting particular HTTP endpoints. Uploading *zip bombs*—corrupt archive files that grow exponentially in size when expanded—to a file upload function can exhaust the server's available disk space. Any URL that performs deserialization—converting the contents of HTTP requests to in-memory code objects—is potentially vulnerable too. One example of this type of attack is an XML bomb, which you looked at in Chapter 15.

Reflected and Amplified Attacks

One difficulty in launching an effective denial-of-service attack is finding enough computing power to generate malicious traffic. Hackers overcome this limitation by using a third-party service to generate the traffic for them. By sending malicious requests to a third party, with a spoofed return address belonging to their intended victim, hackers *reflect* the responses to their target, potentially overwhelming the server responding to traffic at that address. Reflected attacks also disguise the original source of the attack, making them harder to pin down. If the third-party service replies with larger or more numerous responses than the initial request, the larger responses *amplify* the attack power.

One of the largest denial-of-service attacks to date was committed using reflection. A single attacker was able to generate 1.3 terabytes of data *per second* and point it at the GitHub website in 2018. The hacker achieved this by locating a large number of insecure Memcached servers and sending them *User Datagram Protocol (UDP)* requests signed with the IP address of the GitHub servers. Each response was around 50 times larger than the original request, effectively multiplying the attacker's computing power by the same factor.

Distributed Denial-of-Service Attacks

If a denial-of-service attack is launched from a single IP address, it is relatively easy to blacklist traffic from that IP and stop the attack. Modern denial-of-service attacks, such as the 2018 attack on GitHub, come from a multitude of cooperating sources—a *distributed denial-of-service (DDoS)* attack. In addition to using reflection, these attacks are usually launched from a *botnet*, a network of malware bots that have infected various computers and internet-connected devices, and that can be controlled by an attacker. Because many types of devices connect to the internet these days—thermostats, refrigerators, cars, doorbells, hairbrushes—and are prone to having security vulnerabilities, there are a lot of places for these bots to hide.

Unintentional Denial-of-Service Attacks

Not all surges in internet traffic are malicious. It is common to see a website go viral and experience an unexpectedly large number of visitors in a short time, effectively taking it offline for a while because it wasn't built to handle such a high volume of traffic. The Reddit *hug of death* frequently takes smaller websites offline when they manage to reach the front page of the social news site.

Denial-of-Service Attack Mitigation

Defending yourself against a major denial-of-service attack is expensive and time-consuming. Fortunately, you are unlikely to be the target of an attack the size of the one that took Dyn offline in 2016. Such attacks require extensive planning, and only a handful of adversaries would be able to pull them off. You are unlikely to see terabytes of data a second hitting your recipe blog!

However, smaller denial-of-service attacks combined with extortion requests *do* happen, so it pays to put in some safeguards. The following sections describe some of the countermeasures you should consider using: firewalls and intrusion prevention systems, DDoS prevention services, and highly scalable website technologies.

Firewalls and Intrusion Prevention Systems

All modern server operating systems come with a *firewall*—software that monitors and controls incoming and outgoing network traffic based on predetermined security rules. Firewalls allow you to determine which ports should be open to incoming traffic, and to filter out traffic from IP addresses via *access control rules*. Firewalls are placed at the perimeter of an organization's network, to filter out bad traffic before it hits internal servers. Modern firewalls block most ICMP-based attacks and can be used to blacklist individual IP addresses, an effective way of shutting down traffic from a single source.

Application firewalls operate at a higher level of the network stack, acting as proxies that scan HTTP and other internet traffic before it passes to the rest of the network. An application firewall scans incoming traffic for corrupted or malicious requests, and rejects anything that matches a malicious signature. Because signatures are kept up-to-date by vendors, this approach can block many types of hacking attempts (for example, attempts to perform SQL injection), as well as mitigating denial-of-service attacks. In addition to open source implementations such as ModSecurity, commercial application firewall vendors exist (for example, Norton and Barracuda Networks), some of which sell hardware-based solutions.

Intrusion prevention systems (IPSs) take a more holistic approach to protecting a network: in addition to implementing firewalls and matching signatures, they look for statistical anomalies in network traffic and scan files on disk for unusual changes. An IPS is usually a serious investment but can protect you very effectively.

Distributed Denial-of-Service Protection Services

Network packets in a sophisticated denial-of-service attack will usually be indistinguishable from regular packets. The traffic is valid; only the intent and volume of traffic is malicious. This means firewalls cannot filter out the packets.

Numerous companies offer protection against distributed denial-of-service attacks, usually at a significant cost. When you integrate with a DDoS solutions provider, you route all incoming traffic through its data centers, where it scans and blocks anything that looks malicious. Because the solutions provider has a global view of malicious internet activity and a massive amount of available bandwidth, it can use heuristics to prevent any harmful traffic from reaching you.

DDoS protection is often offered by CDNs, because they have geographically dispersed data centers and often already host static content for their clients. If the bulk of your requests are already being served by content hosted on a CDN, it doesn't take too much extra effort to route the remainder of your traffic through its data centers.

Building for Scale

In many ways, being the target of a denial-of-service attack is indistinguishable from having many visitors on your website at once. You can protect yourself against many attempted denial-of-service attacks by being ready to handle large surges in traffic. Building for scale is a big subject—whole books have been written on the topic, and it's an active area of research. Some of the most impactful approaches you should look into are offloading static content, caching database queries, using asynchronous processing for long-running tasks, and deploying to multiple web servers.

CDNs offload the burden of serving static content—such as images and font files—to a third party. Using a CDN significantly improves the responsiveness of your site and reduces the load on your server. CDNs are easy to integrate, cost-efficient for most websites, and will significantly reduce the amount of network requests your web servers have to handle.

Once you offload static content, database access calls typically become the next bottleneck. Effective *caching* can prevent your database from becoming overloaded in the event of a traffic surge. Cached data can be stored on disk, in memory, or in a shared memory cache like Redis or Memcached. Even the browser can help with caching: setting a `Cache-Control` header on a resource (for example, an image) tells the browser to store a local copy of the resource and not request it again until a configurable future date.

Offloading long-running tasks to a *job queue* will help your web server respond quickly when traffic ramps up. This is an approach to web architecture that moves long-running jobs (such as generating large download files or sending email) to background *worker* processes. These workers are deployed separately from the web server, which creates the jobs and puts them on the queue. The workers take jobs off the queue and handle them one at a time, notifying the web server when the job is completed. Have a look at the Netflix technology blog (*https://medium.com/@NetflixTechBlog/*) for an example of a massively scalable system built on this type of principle.

Finally, you should have a deployment strategy that allows you to scale out the number of web servers relatively quickly, so you can ramp up your computing power during busy periods. An Infrastructure as a Service (IaaS) provider like Amazon Web Services (AWS) makes it easy to deploy the same server image multiple times behind a load balancer. Platforms like Heroku make it as simple as moving a slider on their web dashboard! Your hosting provider will have some method of monitoring traffic volume, and tools like Google Analytics can be used to track when and how many sessions are open on your site. Then you need only to increase the number of servers when monitoring thresholds are hit.

Summary

Attackers use denial-of-service attacks to make a site unavailable to legitimate users by flooding it with a large volume of traffic. Denial-of-service attacks can happen at any layer of the network stack, and can be reflected or amplified by third-party services. Frequently, they are launched as a distributed attack from a botnet controlled by the attacker.

Simple denial-of-service attacks can be defused by sensible firewall settings. Application firewalls and intrusion prevention systems help protect you against more-sophisticated attacks. The most comprehensive (and hence most expensive) protection comes from distributed denial-of-service attack solution providers, which will filter out all bad traffic before it hits your network.

All types of denial-of-service attacks—including inadvertent ones, when you suddenly see a surge of new visitors—can be mitigated by building your site to scale well. Content delivery networks alleviate the burden of serving static content from your site, and effective caching prevents your database from being a bottleneck. Moving long-running processes to a job queue will keep your web servers running efficiently at full capacity. Active traffic monitoring, and the ability to easily scale up the number of web servers, will prepare you well for busy periods.

That concludes all the individual vulnerabilities you will be looking at in this book! The final chapter summarizes the major security principles covered over the course of the book and recaps the individual vulnerabilities and how to protect against them.

18

SUMMING UP

So, we reach the end of the book! We covered a lot of material, but you should now feel like you are ready to go out in the world and build websites in a safe, secure manner.

Let's finish with a brief recap. This chapter presents 21 commandments of web security that will help you remember the key lessons from each chapter. Follow these simple steps, and the likelihood of you being hacked will be close to zero.

Automate Your Release Process

Be able to build your code from a single command line call. Keep your code in source control and decide on a branching strategy. Separate configuration from code, so it is easy to build testing environments. Use a testing environment to validate functionality before each release. Automate the deployment of code to each environment. Make sure your release process is reliable, reproducible, and revertible. Always know which version of the code is running on each environment, and be able to roll back to a prior version in a simple fashion.

Do (Thorough) Code Reviews

Make sure every code change is reviewed by at least one team member who is not the original author before it is approved for release. Ensure that team members have time to critically assess code changes, and understand that reviewing code is just as important as writing it.

Test Your Code (to the Point of Boredom)

Write unit tests to make assertions about critical sections of your codebase, and run them as part of your build process. Run your unit tests on a continuous integration server with each change. Measure the percentage of your codebase that is executed when unit tests are run, and always try to increase this coverage number. Write tests to reproduce software bugs *before* fixing the bug. Test until fear turns into boredom!

Anticipate Malicious Input

All parts of the HTTP request will be manipulated by hackers, so be ready. Construct queries to databases and the operating system by using parameterized statements so you are protected against injection attacks.

Neutralize File Uploads

If your users can upload files to your website, make sure those files cannot be executed. Ideally, upload files to a content delivery network (CDN). If you need more fine-grained permissions for files, host them in a content management system (CMS). As a last resort, save uploaded files in a separate disk partition and make sure they are not written to disk with executable permissions.

Escape Content While Writing HTML

Attackers will attempt to inject malicious JavaScript in your web pages by smuggling JavaScript into your database or hiding it in HTTP parameters. Make sure any dynamic content written to your web pages is escaped—replace HTML control characters with safe entity encodings. This applies on the client side as well as the server side! If possible, disable the execution of inline JavaScript altogether by using the `Content-Security-Policy` response header.

Be Suspicious of HTTP Requests from Other Sites

HTTP requests originating from other domains may be malicious—for instance, an attacker may have tricked one of your users into clicking a disguised link. Make sure `GET` requests to your site are side-effect free: they should be used only to retrieve resources. Ensure that other types of requests (such as `POST` requests used to initiate login) originate from your site by incorporating anti-forgery cookies in your HTML forms and any HTTP requests initiated by JavaScript. Strip cookies from requests initiated outside your web domain by adding the `SameSite` attribute to your `Set-Cookie` HTTP response header.

Hash and Salt Your Passwords

If you store passwords in your database, encrypt them with a strong, one-way hash function such as `bcrypt` before saving them. Add an element of randomness to each hash by adding a salt.

Don't Admit Who Your Users Are

The only person who should know whether a user has signed up to your site is the user themselves. Make sure login forms and password reset pages do not permit a hacker to mine your site for a list of users: keep error and information messages generic, whether a username exists or not.

Protect Your Cookies

If an attacker can steal your cookies, they can hijack your users' identities. Add the HttpOnly keyword to your Set-Cookie response headers so cookies cannot be read by malicious JavaScript. Add the Secure keyword so that cookies are sent only over HTTPS.

Protect Sensitive Resources (Even If You Don't Link to Them)

Check that a user has permissions to access any sensitive resource on your site before returning it in an HTTP request—even if that resource isn't listed in search pages or linked to from elsewhere.

Avoid Using Direct File References

Avoid passing and evaluating file paths in HTTP requests. Use your web server's built-in URL resolution for evaluating paths to resources, or refer to files by opaque identifiers.

Don't Leak Information

Minimize the amount of information an attacker can learn about your tech stack. Turn off any Server header in your HTTP responses and make sure your session parameter name is generic in your Set-Cookie header. Avoid telltale file suffixes in URLs. Make sure to turn off detailed client-side error reporting in your production environment. Obfuscate the JavaScript libraries you used during your build process.

Use Encryption (Correctly)

Purchase a security certificate for your domain and install it on your web server along with your private encryption key. Divert all traffic to HTTPS, and add the Secure keyword to your Set-Cookie response header to ensure that cookies are never sent over unencrypted HTTP. Update your web server regularly to keep on top of encryption standards.

Secure Your Dependencies (and Services)

Use a package manager to import third-party code during the build process and fix each package to a specific version number. Keep on top of security advisories for the packages you use and update them regularly. Store your configuration securely—outside source control! Use the SafeFrame standard for any advertisements you host.

Defuse Your XML Parser

Turn off processing of inline document type declarations in your XML parser.

Send Email Securely

Whitelist which servers are permitted to send email from your domain by using a Sender Policy Framework (SPF) record in your domain records.

Allow mail recipients to verify the `From` address of any email you send and to detect attempts to tamper with an email by using DomainKeys Identified Mail (DKIM).

Check Your Redirects (If You Have Any)

If you redirect to a URL stored in part of the HTTP request—for example, after a user logs in—check that the URL is local to your domain rather than an external website. Otherwise, these open redirects will be used to disguise malicious links in emails.

Don't Allow Your Site to Be Framed

Don't allow your website to be enclosed in an `<iframe>` unless you have a specific need to do so. Disable framing by adding `Content-Security-Policy: frame-ancestors 'none'` to your HTTP responses.

Lock Down Your Permissions

Follow the principle of least privilege—ensure that each process and software component runs with the minimum number of permissions required. Think through what an attacker might try to do if they compromise any part of your system, and mitigate the harm. Ensure that your web server process is not running as a root operating system account. Limit the directories on disk that your web server can access. Prevent unnecessary network calls from your web server. Have your web server connect to your database under an account with limited permissions.

Detect and Be Ready for Surges in Traffic

Use real-time monitoring to detect high traffic volumes to your website. Build for scale by using a CDN, client-side cookies, caching, and asynchronous processing. Be able to easily scale up the number of servers hosting your site. If malicious traffic becomes a problem, deploy a firewall or intrusion prevention system, or consider signing up for distributed-denial-of-service protection.

INDEX

Page numbers followed by an italicized *f* or *t* refer to figures and tables respectively.

CMSs. *See* content management systems (CMSs)

CNAME (canonical name) records, 9

code reviews, 38, 170

code writing phase (in the software development lifecycle)
    branching and merging code, 38
    pushing changes to repository, 37
    source control (version control), 37

CoffeeScript, 34, 42

colon character (:), 82

Comcast, 128

command injection attacks
    anatomy of, 56–57, 57*f*
    defined, 56
    escaping control characters, 57–58
    file upload vulnerability and, 61

Common Gateway Interface (CGI), xxii

Common Language Runtime (CLR), 33

Comodo, 122

Completely Automated Public Turing test to tell Computers and Humans Apart (CAPTCHA), 91–92, 92*f*, 158

CONNECT requests (in TCP), 11*t*

consistent behavior
    eventual consistency of NoSQL databases, 30
    SQL databases, 29

containerization, 42

content delivery networks (CDNs), 26
    distributed denial-of-service protect systems, 167
    mitigating file upload vulnerability attacks, 62, 170
    subdomain takeovers, 140

content management systems (CMSs)
    defined, 26
    mitigating file upload vulnerability attacks, 62, 170
    plug-ins, 26
    vulnerabilities of, 26, 27*f*

content security policies, 69–70, 110–111

Content-Security-Policy header, 69, 158–159, 172

Content-Type header, 13, 59, 63

continuous integration servers, 39

control characters
    in PHP, 56–58
    in SQL, 51–53, 55

Cookie header, 13, 77–78, 97

cookies, 171
    anti-CSRF cookies, 77–78
    defined, 13
    digital signing of, 96–97
    generic cookie parameters, 114
    implementing and securing a logout function, 90–91
    SameSite cookie attribute, 78–79
    session cookies, 95–97, 114
    session hijacking, 97–99
    vulnerabilities of, 13

cookie theft
    cross-site request forgery (CSRF) attacks, 98–99
    cross-site scripting (XSS) attacks, 97–98
    man-in-the-middle attacks, 98

cracking password lists, 89

CREATE statements (in SQL), 55

cross-site request forgery (CSRF; XSRF) attacks
    anatomy of, 76
    cookie theft, 98–99
    defined, 75
    mitigation options
        anti-CSRF cookies, 77–78
        requiring reauthentication for sensitive actions, 78–79
        REST principles, 76–77
        SameSite cookie attribute, 78–79

cross-site scripting (XSS) attacks, xxi, 19
    cookie theft, 97–98
    defined, 65
    DOM-based
        defined, 71
        escaping dynamic content, 73
        URI fragments, 71–73
    reflected, 70–71
        defined, 70
        escaping dynamic content, 71
    stored
        content security policies, 69–70
        escaping control characters, 67–69
        example of, 66–67, 66*f*–67*f*

cryptographic hash algorithms and functions, 88–89, 119

cryptography, 117

File Transfer Protocol (FTP)
  defined, 10
  Internet Protocol suite layers, 10*f*
file upload vulnerability attacks
  anatomy of, 60–61, 61*f*
  defined, 60
  file upload functions, defined, 60
  mitigation options, 61–63, 170
    ensuring uploaded files cannot
      be executed, 62
    hosting files on secure system, 62
    running antivirus software, 63
    validating content of uploaded
      files, 63
firewalls, 166
Flask, 125
foreign keys (in SQL), 29
four eyes principle, 38
FTP. *See* File Transfer Protocol (FTP)
fully qualified domain names
  (FQDNs), 123

G

Galois/Counter Mode (GCM), 121
GET requests (in HTTP), 11, 49–50
  cross-site request forgery attacks,
    76–77
  rendering pipeline, 20
  SameSite attribute settings for
    cookies, 99
Git, 37–38
GitHub, 37–38, 136, 163, 165
GitHub OAuth, 84
Google
  Angular framework, 33–34
  government snooping, 129
  HTTP requests, 70
  reCAPTCHA widget, 92
  returning dynamic resources, 27
Google AdSense, 138, 141–143
Google AdX, 142
Google Analytics, 26, 140–141, 168
Google App Engine, 41
Google Apps, 70
Google Chrome, xxi, 83*f*
  cipher suites, 121
  V8 JavaScript engine, 32
Google Hacking Database, 136
Google OAuth, 84
Google Safe Browsing API, 158

government agencies, snooping by, 129
gzip algorithm, 25

H

Hacker News, 135
hacking
  black hat hackers, 2
  dark web, 2, 2*f*
  exploits, defined, 1
  process for, 3–4
  white hat hackers, 2
  zero-day exploits, 2
hardening servers, 62
hashed values, 88, 119–120
hashes, 171
  digest authentication scheme, 82
  hashing passwords, 88, 119–120
  salting hashes, 89, 171
headers
  in HTTP requests, 10–11
  in HTTP responses, 12–13, 25
HEAD requests (in HTTP), 11*t*
Heartbleed bug, 132
Heartland Payment Systems, 50
Heroku, 41, 168
horizontal escalation, 104
hosting services, 110–111
HSTS (HTTP Strict Transport
  Security) policies, 126–127
HTML. *See* HyperText Markup
  Language (HTML)
HTTP. *See* HyperText Transfer Protocol
  (HTTP)
HTTP 404 Not Found error, 13
HttpOnly keyword, 97–98, 171
HTTP requests, 170–171
  authentication, 82
  command injection attacks, 56–58
  CONNECT requests, 11*t*
  cross-site request forgery attacks, 76
  defined, 10
  DELETE requests, 11
  elements of
    body, 10
    headers, 10–11
    methods (verbs), 10–11
    universal resource locators,
      10–11
  example of, 10–11
  exploit scripts, 59

vulnerabilities of
  government agencies, 129
  Internet service providers,
    128–129
  Wi-Fi hotspots, 128
  wireless routers, 128
web servers, 23–25, 27

I

IaaS (Infrastructure as a Service), 41, 168
ICANN (Internet Corporation for
    Assigned Names and
    Numbers), 8
ICMP (Internet Control Message
    Protocol) attacks, 164
identity and access management (IAM)
    system, 105
<iframe> tags, 142, 158, 172
images (configuration scripts), 42
indirection, 111
infinite scrolling, 72
information leaks, 171
  mitigation options, 113–116
    disabling client-side error
      reporting, 115
    disabling telltale Server
      headers, 114
    minifying or obfuscating
      JavaScript files, 115
    sanitizing client-side files, 116
    use generic cookie
      parameters, 114
    using clean URLs, 114
  security advisories, 116
  zero-day vulnerabilities, 112
Infrastructure as a Service (IaaS), 41, 168
injection attacks, xxii
  anticipating, 170
  client-server vulnerabilities, 49–50
  command injection attacks
    anatomy of, 56–57, 57f
    defined, 56
    escaping control characters,
      57–58
  defined, 49
  file upload vulnerability attacks
    anatomy of, 60–61, 61f
    defined, 60
    ensuring uploaded files cannot
      be executed, 62
    hosting files on secure system, 62

running antivirus software, 63
  validating content of uploaded
    files, 63
remote code execution attacks
  anatomy of, 59
  defined, 59
  disabling code-execution
    during deserialization,
    59–60
SQL injection attacks
  anatomy of, 51–52
  defense in depth, 55–56
  object-relational mapping,
    54–55
  parameterized statements,
    52–53
  SQL, defined, 50–51
INSERT statements (in SQL), 50–51, 55
integration testing, 39
integrity checkers, 134, 160
internal entity declarations, 148
internet, history of, xx–xxiii
Internet Control Message Protocol
    (ICMP) attacks, 164
Internet Corporation for Assigned
    Names and Numbers
    (ICANN), 8
Internet Protocol (IP)
  encryption algorithms, 118–119
  hash functions, 119–120
  message authentication codes, 120
  TLS handshakes, 120–122
Internet Protocol (IP) addresses
  allotment of, 8
  defined, 8
  IP version 4 (IPv4) syntax, 8–9
  IP version 6 (IPv6) syntax, 9
  rendering pipeline, 20
Internet Protocol suite
  defined, 8–9
  Domain Name System, 9
  HyperText Transfer Protocol, 10–13
    encryption, 14
    stateful connections, 13
  Internet Protocol addresses, 8–9
  layers of, 9–10, 10f
  Transmission Control Protocol, 8
  User Datagram Protocol, 8
Internet service providers (ISPs), 8,
    128–129
Intrusion prevention systems (IPSs), 166

message authentication codes
(MACs), 120
Metasploit framework, 3–4, *3f,* 52, 114
<meta> tags, 69
methods (verbs) in HTTP, 10–11
MFA. *See* multifactor
authentication (MFA)
microframeworks, 31
microservices
defined, 30
distributed caches, 30
publish-subscribe channels, 31
queues, 30
Microsoft
dedicated configuration store, 137
operating system patches, 135
third-party authentication, 84
Microsoft Active Directory, 105–106
Microsoft Azure, 41
Microsoft Internet Explorer, xiii
Microsoft Windows, xiii
minifying JavaScript files, 42–43, 115
MODIFY statements (in SQL), 55
MongoDB, 53
monitoring, 44
Mono project, 33
Mosaic, xiii
Mozilla Firefox, xiii
Mozilla Foundation, 125
multifactor authentication (MFA)
requiring, 89–90, *90f*
third-party authentication, 84
MX (mail exchange) records, 9, 86

N

National Center for Supercomputing
Applications, xiii
National Security Agency (NSA), 129
.NET, 33
dependency checker, 136
securing XML parsers, 151
Netflix
denial-of-service attacks, 163
technology blog, 168
Netgear, 128
Netscape, xiii, 95
Nginx, 125–126, 132
Node.js, 32, 133, 136, 151
Node Package Manager (NPM), 136
nonblind SQL injection attacks, 55
NoSQL databases, 30, 53

npm audit command, 136
NSA (National Security Agency), 129
nslookup command, 56–57

O

OAuth (open authentication) standard,
84, 158
obfuscating JavaScript files, 115
object-relational mapping (ORM),
54–55
Offensive Security, 3, 136
offloading static content, 167
Okta, 84
OneLogin, 84
opaque IDs, 108, 111, 171
open authentication (OAuth) standard,
84, 158
open directory listings, disabling, 137
OpenID standard, 84
open redirects, 153, 156–157, 172
OpenSSL, 132
openssl tool, 124–125
Open Web Application Security Project
(OWASP), 136
operating system patches, 133–134
OPTIONS requests (in HTTP), 11*t*
Oracle VirtualBox, 3
ORM (object-relational mapping),
54–55
os module (in Python), 62
OWASP (Open Web Application
Security Project), 136
ownership-based access control, 106

P

PaaS (Platform as a Service), 41
padding input data, 119
parameterized statements, 52–53
parent directories, 109, 112
password-reset links, 87
password-reset screens, 91
passwords. *See also* authentication
commonly used, 84
cracking password lists, 89
hashing, 88–89, 119–120
requiring complex, 87–88
securely storing
hashes, 88–89
salting hashes, 89
securing resets, 87, 171

Secure Hash Algorithm (SHA-256), 121
Secure keyword, 98
Security Assertion Markup Language
    (SAML), 85
security certificates, 20
security through obscurity, 108
seeds, 100
segregation of test and production
    environments, 39
SELECT statements (in SQL), 50–51,
    53, 55
self-signed certificates, 124–125
semicolon character (;), 52
Sender Policy Framework (SPF),
    155–156, 172
SendGrid, 138, 156
sequence numbers, 8
serialization, 59
serialization libraries, 59–60
Server header (in HTTP responses),
    114, 171
server-side request forgery (SSRF)
    attacks, 150, 154, 159–160
server-side sessions, 94–95
session cookies, 95–97
    cookie theft, 97–99
    generic cookie parameters, 114
session fixation, 99–100
session hijacking
    client-side sessions, 96–97
    cookie theft, 97–99
    defined, 93
    opening sessions, 94
    server-side sessions, 94–95
    session fixation, 99–100
    weak session IDs, 100
session identifiers (session IDs)
    session cookies, 95–99
    taking advantage of weak, 100
    TLS handshakes, 121
    URL rewriting, 99–100
session keys, 121–122
session state, 94–96
Set-Cookie header, 13, 20, 77–78,
    90–91, 95–98, 171
SHA-256 (Secure Hash Algorithm), 121
SharkLasers, 87f
Simple Mail Transport Protocol
    (SMTP), 154–155
    defined, 10
    Internet Protocol suite layers, 10f

single-page apps, 72
single quote character ('), 51–53
single sign-on (SSO), 84–85
Slowloris attack, 165
smoke testing. *See* post-release testing
SMTP. *See* Simple Mail Transfer
    Protocol (SMTP)
Snowden, Edward, 129
social media
    database storage, 28, 66
    likejacking, 158
    logout function, 90
    ownership-based access control, 106
    permissions, 103–104, 106–107
    posting links to external URLs, 158
    SameSite attribute settings for
        cookies, 99
    security advisories, 135
    third-party authentication, 84
software development kits (SDKs)
    avoiding server-side request forgery
        attacks, 160
    defined, 31
Software Development Life
    Cycle (SDLC)
    code writing
        branching and merging code, 38
        pushing changes to repository, 37
        source control, 37
    defined, 36
    design and analysis, 36
    post-release testing and
        observation, 43–45
        error reporting, 44–45
        logging, 44–45
        monitoring, 44
        penetration testing, 44
    pre-release testing
        continuous integration
            servers, 39
        coverage, 39
        manual testing, 38
        test environments, 39–40
        unit testing, 39
    release process, 40–43
        build process, 42–43
        database migration scripts, 43
        DevOps tools, 41–42
        Infrastructure as a Service, 41
        Platform as a Service, 41

source control (version control)
    defined, 37
        distributed vs. centralized, 37
        pull requests, 38
Space Jam website, 24
spam email and filters, 105, 154, 160
spearphishing, 154
SPF (Sender Policy Framework),
        155–156, 172
Splunk, 45
spoofing, 50, 123, 153
Spotify, 163
SQL. *See* Structured Query
        Language (SQL)
SQL injection attacks
    anatomy of, 51–52
    defined, 50
    mitigation options
        defense in depth, 55–56
        object-relational mapping, 54–55
        parameterized statements, 52–53
    SQL, defined, 50–51
SSO (single sign-on), 84–85
SSRF (server-side request forgery)
        attacks, 150, 154, 159–160
Stack Overflow, 138
staging environments. *See* test
        environments
Stanford University, 7
stateful connections, 13
static resources
    content delivery networks, 26
    content management systems, 26, 27f
    defined, 24
    URL resolution, 24–25
status codes, 12–13
status messages, 12
stored cross-site scripting attacks
    content security policies, 69–70
    escaping control characters, 67–69
    example of, 66–67, 66f–67f
Stripe, 138
Structured Query Language (SQL)
    databases, 29–30, 105
    defined, 29, 50
    typical statements, 50–51
<style> tags, 17, 134
styling rules and information (in CSS)
    build process, 43
    defined, 16
    rendering pipeline, 16–18

subresource integrity checks, 134
symmetric encryption algorithms, 119
SYN floods, 164
system() function (in PHP), 58

T

TCP. *See* Transmission Control
        Protocol (TCP)
templates, xiv
    dynamic resources, 28
    stored cross-site scripting attacks,
        68–69
test coverage, 39
test environments (staging, pre-
        production, or quality
        assurance environments)
    close resemblance to production
        environment, 39–40
    defined, 39
    hardening, 138
    scrubbed data for, 40
    segregation production
        environment and, 40
testing
    integration testing, 39
    penetration testing, 44, 160
    post-release, 43–45
    pre-release, 38–40
    regression testing, 135
    unit testing, 39, 107, 170
third-party authentication, 84
third-party code
    securing configuration, 136–138
        disabling default credentials, 137
        disabling open directory
            listings, 137
        hardening test
            environments, 138
        protecting configuration
            information, 137–138
        securing administrative
            frontends, 138
    securing dependencies, 132–136, 171
        deploying new versions
            quickly, 134
        organizing dependencies,
            132–134
        staying alert to security issues,
            135–136
        timely upgrades, 136